ORDEAL BELOW ZERO

By the same author

BORN TO FLY
*Exploits of the War's Great
Fighter Aces*

THE HEROIC STORY OF THE
ARCTIC CONVOYS IN WORLD WAR II

ORDEAL BELOW ZERO

BY
GEORGES BLOND

SOUVENIR PRESS

To the memory of Frederick William Charles Thomson,
known to his shipmates as Duke,
22 February 1921 – 13 February 2015.
A veteran of convoys JW64 and RA65

Copyright © 1956 by Georges Blond

First published in Great Britain in 1956 by Souvenir Press Ltd
43 Great Russell Street, London WC1B 3PD

This paperback edition 2018

The right of Georges Blond to be identified as the author of this work has
been asserted in accordance with section 77 of the Copyright, Designs and
Patents Act, 1988

ISBN   9780285643833

Printed and bound in Denmark by Nørhaven, Viborg

Contents

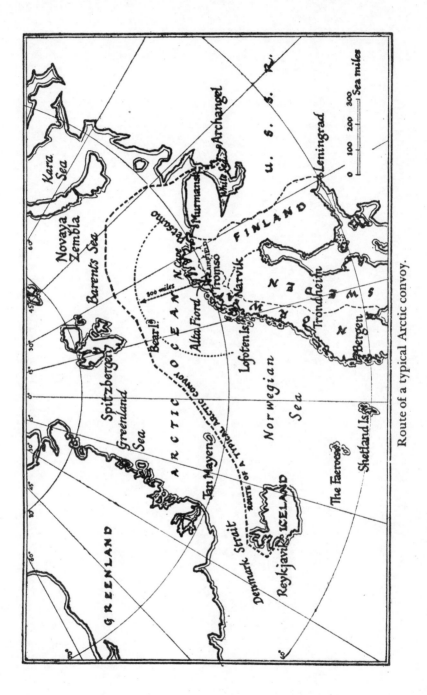

Route of a typical Arctic convoy.

Foreword

EARLY IN OCTOBER, 1941, THE BEAVERBROOK·
Harriman Mission to Moscow conceived and agreed one
of the most brilliant and hazardous operations of the war:
the delivery of vital materials by sea to North Russia.
Beginning immediately, regular convoys of escorted merchant ships, having assembled in Scottish ports or at
Reykjavik in Iceland, crossed the Arctic Ocean carrying
explosives, arms and ammunition, vehicles, petrol, tanks
and aircraft, as well as food and publicly donated Red
Cross supplies, to the Russian ports of Murmansk, Archangel and Molotovsk.

They sailed through the Arctic darkness, in ice, fog,
blizzards and mountainous seas, unable to avoid passing
near the German airfields in occupied Norway. Some of the
convoys were attacked almost throughout the voyage, for
eight to ten days without interruption, by altitude and dive
bombers, torpedo carrying aircraft, packs of U-boats and
surface vessels.

One of them, for which an escort had been detailed
of two 35,000-ton battleships, an aircraft carrier, seven
cruisers, eighteen destroyers, a score of corvettes and small
escorting craft, was finally dispersed 240 miles north of
the North Cape, the merchant ships receiving orders to
proceed individually as best they could to the Russian
ports. Out of thirty-three ships, eleven reached their destination ; the remaining twenty-two were sunk. Some shipwrecked crews picked up by other vessels, only to be
shipwrecked once more, coasted for weeks along the icy
barren shores of Novaya Zemlya, with frost-bitten feet and
half dead with hunger. " Nothing like this has ever been
seen in our maritime history," wrote a British historian.

The survivors of these voyages were compelled to return by the same route to reach Iceland or Scotland. Some of the ships which had got through on the outward journey were sunk on the way home or were blown up by mines. A number of the sailors in these tankers or merchantmen were subjected to such ordeals that they afterwards required treatment in nerve hospitals or special rest centres. I have tried to set down, as far as it has been possible, what happened to these men and their ships. I have also described the actions of the escort vessels, whose task was a grim one, with some account of the main air-sea operations which took place in the defence of the convoys.

For general information on the convoys, the chronology and outcome of the operations, I am fortunate enough to have had direct or indirect access to official sources. The rest has been reconstructed from the testimony of merchant seamen. I am fully aware that these accounts, published during or immediately after the war in British and American magazines and newspapers (particularly the American), were sometimes frowned upon by official historians at a period when it was necessary to keep up the morale of the civilian population. They seem no less interesting to me on this account. The reality of war does not entirely consist of military campaign, acts of courage and self-sacrifice; it also includes anxiety, fear, discouragement and revolt.

The Arctic convoys were entrusted to the Royal Navy but after January, 1942, they included American cargo ships and tankers, which were sometimes in the majority. There were occasionally a few Russian ships. From April to July, 1942, U.S. naval forces participated in the escort and air cover of the convoys.

For security reasons the names of the vessels were withheld in the wartime accounts; later some, but not all, of them were published. Cross-checking has enabled me to determine in which convoy a particular ship sailed and to give its itinerary. In the following pages, whenever the name of a ship is quoted, it is historically correct. When there is any question of doubt I merely refer to " a cargo vessel " or " a tanker "; no ship's name has been invented. The names of the sailors were sometimes given in the documents and in newspaper articles, sometimes not, and I have done the same.

It is unlikely that anyone who sailed on the Arctic convoys will ever forget them. The seamen, the gunners, the pilots, were drawn from all walks of life, regular servicemen and men who had left their shops and offices and factories to venture across the roof of the world in the teeth of winter and of everything that the enemy could hurl at them.

This is their story.

CHAPTER ONE

Start Point

AT THE BEGINNING OF MAY, 1942, MOST OF the merchant ships comprising convoy PQ 16, destined for Murmansk and Archangel, were assembled in readiness at Greenock. Among their crews was a Norwegian sailor whose identity remains unknown. His mates called him Sven. Sven passed the Straits of Gibraltar in the spring of 1941 in a British cargo boat, part of a convoy bound for Alexandria. How his journey ended is a story worth telling.

The convoy was first attacked for twelve hours by Heinkel 111s, Stukas, Macchi Ma 220s and Savoia Marchetti S 79s. Sven lost his hearing while at his action station on the bridge, on the look-out for U-boats (the bombs rained down but the submarines were still very much in evidence) ; an explosion blew him overboard ; he found himself on his back in the sea, kept afloat by his lifebelt. Struggling for breath, he retained a vivid impression of the stern of the vessel as it rose in the air, its screws still slowly turning.

The Norwegian struck out away from the ship so as not to be sucked down, making his way through the floating wreckage and bodies. Luckily, he was picked up almost immediately; a destroyer loomed alongside and he seized its large meshed net and clambered painfully inboard. Some of the crew took him to the mess, sat him down and handed him a tot of rum. But he did not drink; laying his head on his folded arms, he fell asleep. A little later he was woken up by the sound of the destroyer's ack-ack guns in action. Presently a sailor ran in shouting " Look out!" and the next instant both men were hurled head

15

first on to the mess deck. The lamps went out. Sven scrambled to his feet and, summoning his last reserve of strength, groped his way aloft. He remembered that with pounding heart he had run along the listing deck of the warship and found himself once more in the sea. Then he fainted.

After a time which he had no means of measuring, he realised that he was in a hospital bed, a shaft of sunlight lighting up a white-washed ceiling above him. Outside, guns were firing. Feeling a hand on his shoulder, he turned his head to find a nurse looking down at him. " Those who can walk," she said in English, " must get up and dress. We haven't enough staff to carry all the wounded down into the shelters." Sven obeyed as though in a dream. " Where am I? " he asked.

" Valetta," she replied. " In Malta. You've been suffering from shock."

Following the other wounded men able to walk, Sven was led out of the town into the open country. While the harbour was being bombed, the men lay in a field wrapped up in blankets, Sven on his back looking up at the sky. He could hear the sound of gunfire and the drone of engines, but he did not want to think of all that; he was watching the stars appear in the sky, each at its appointed time and place as though the folly of mankind had not existed. At dawn the bombing ceased and the men were taken back through the ruins to their hospital.

Sven remained a few days in Malta, experienced several more bombing attacks, and was then flown by ambulance aircraft to Cairo and later to Gibraltar. A hospital ship brought him back to England where he was given medical attention. After a period of convalescence he signed on again in a cargo boat. This ship, bound for the Persian Gulf, was torpedoed off the Cape of Good Hope. Sven spent twenty days in a life boat with seventeen other sailors, ten of whom died. He had survived once more.

Also in one of the ships under orders to sail from Greenock was an American, Davis Doyle. He had embarked in June, 1941, in the *Robin Moor*, the first of the ships loaned to Great Britain by the United States under lease-lend. The *Robin Moor* was torpedoed off Freetown, Sierra Leone. Picked up by an escort vessel and taken on board an English cargo boat of the convoy, Doyle reached Basra in the Persian Gulf without incident. He was shipwrecked a second time, however, on the homeward journey, eighty miles off Saint Vincent, Cape Verde. Yet again he survived.

Another sailor, an Englishman, Paul Jordan, a member of the crew of the *Lowther Castle*, now waiting to leave for Murmansk, had been on board a British ship sunk by the *Graf Spee* on December 7th, 1940, 1,160 miles off Rio de Janeiro. With twenty-nine of his shipmates, he had been picked up by this pirate. They remained aboard for a week, sharing the indifferent food of the German sailors and their chronic lack of space. On the morning of the 13th December, Jordan was present at the historic action between the *Graf Spee* and the British cruisers, *H.M.S. Exeter, Ajax* and *Achilles*. Locked in a watertight compartment without porthole, the prisoners could feel by the vibration that the battle-cruiser was sailing at full speed; for several hours, without the slightest idea of what was happening outside, they discussed whether the terrible buffetings received by the *Graf Spee* were caused by the firing of her salvoes or by direct hits from allied warships. At midnight the pirate stopped and a German officer visited the prisoners. " We are at anchor off Montevideo," he said. " You will be released tomorrow." With a lamentable ignorance of the future he added, " The war is over for you."

The first convoy destined for the Russian Arctic ports had set sail from Scotland in August, 1941. On the orders and official documents the individual convoys were known by the letters PQ: PQ 1, 2, 3 etc., and those returning from Russia by the letters QP.

Before August, 1941, the two maritime routes used by

17

Great Britain and the United States in their relations with the U.S.S.R. were the transpacific U.S.-Vladivostok and the Persian Gulf route. Along the first sailed the American and Russian ships; after the attack on Pearl Harbour only the Russians; although they were loaded with American material the Japanese, not wishing the Russians to declare war on them, let them through. But the quays and sheds of Vladivostok were soon filled to overflowing, for the thin endless line of the Trans-Siberian Railway limited traffic by this route.

On the Persian Gulf route the convoys sailing from the British ports met those from the American Atlantic seaboard. Since the Mediterranean was to all intents and purposes closed in the centre, both of them went round the Cape. From the American ports to the Persian Gulf is about 14,500 miles; a seventy-three days' run. Other convoys sailing from the same Atlantic ports used the Panama Canal, crossing the Pacific and the Indian Ocean: 18,000 miles.

The cargoes were unloaded at Basra and Hormuz and then transported to the U.S.S.R. by the Iranian railway. Delivery had been speeded up at the cost of extensive works and enormous expense: all the material, including the cranes, locomotives and trucks, could only arrive by the Cape route or after crossing the Pacific and the Indian Oceans.

Despite their expansion, the quays of Basra and Hormuz were soon chronically overstrained. For lack of warehousing space, ships were obliged to return and unload at Karachi, where material also began to pile up. Each kilo which reached the U.S.S.R. cost a fortune, particularly since this ant-like odyssey by the longest maritime routes in the world necessitated the use of an excessive number of vessels.

The early convoys got through and returned without being attacked, except by pure chance. At the outset the Germans had no idea of the importance of the cargoes carried: for the first four months 100,000 tons of material:

600 tanks, 800 aircraft and 1,400 vehicles. The Luftwaffe alerted them by reporting more and more British warships in the Arctic Ocean. At first Hitler thought that an attack on Norway was imminent; then the reports informed him that the warships were escorting and protecting convoys. These became of interest. The 35,000-ton battleship *Tirpitz*, the 10,000-ton pocket battleship *Admiral Scheer*, the 10,000-ton heavy cruiser *Admiral Hipper* and the 10,000-ton pocket battleship *Lützow* were despatched to Norway in January, February, March and May respectively. The aircraft based on Norway and Finland was considerably reinforced.

On the evening of March 5th, 1942, Admiral Raeder's Chief of Staff handed him a decoded telegram from the German air base of Bardufloss, situated between Narvik and Tromsö. The substance of the message was: *Enemy convoy, fifteen merchant ships escorted by a cruiser and four destroyers or corvettes, sighted seventy miles south of Jan Mayen Island, sailing north. Our reconnaissance aircraft are trying to maintain contact.* Jan Mayen is a deserted volcanic island, a Norwegian possession, positioned about Long. 10° W. on the same parallel as Scoresby Sound, Greenland.

Having read the message, Admiral Raeder issued his orders without hesitation. A signal was sent immediately to Vice-Admiral Otto Ciliax on board the *Tirpitz* at Trondhjem: *Put to sea to intercept and destroy the convoy reported.* A second message went to the O.C. Narvik base: six U-boats were to take up their position east of the North Cape with orders to sink any ships that escaped the battleship.

The convoy reported was the PQ 12; its importance and the composition of its escort had been very accurately observed by the German airmen. This accuracy was all the more meritorious as an almost uninterrupted gale had been blowing in the North Atlantic since the beginning of February, and further north there was fog.

No German reconnaissance plane had spotted the presence of the " covering force " which was cruising between Iceland and Norway to protect the convoy PQ 12 and the QP 8 returning from Murmansk. This force consisted of the 35,000-ton battleship *H.M.S. King George V* in which Admiral Sir Jack Tovey, C. in C. Home Fleet, flew his flag; the 23,000-ton aircraft carrier *H.M.S. Victorious,* and nine destroyers.

The *Tirpitz* emerged from the Trondhjem narrows on the 6th March, escorted by three destroyers and covered in the air by Luftwaffe aircraft based at Trondhjem. But during the morning Bardufloss announced that its reconnaissance planes could not remain airborne in such weather and were returning to base.

The *Tirpitz* was a 35,000-ton battleship, 783 feet overall and 120 feet in the beam; when she pitched, the angry grey sea broke over her bows, reaching the gun turrets; the bridge ports were covered with spray. The sight afforded by the three destroyers, one ahead and one on each beam, was even more impressive ; they pitched until their keels could be seen. The " attacking force " was sailing approximately N.N.E. towards the estimated position of the convoy.

Above, the sky was white; in all directions the horizon seemed to smoke. Several times that day Vice-Admiral Ciliax asked the battleship commander if he thought that catapulting an aircraft was feasible (the *Tirpitz* carried two catapults and four aircraft).

The Captain replied that the pilots were at his disposal, without adding another word, and the Admiral did not give the orders for them to be launched.

Night came, transforming the visible world into a black moaning chaos. From the bridges of the destroyers, the officers on watch barely caught a glimpse of the long silhouette of the battleship, wallowing heavily. At dawn the attacking force changed its course to the north. It still seemed impossible to catapult aircraft. Towards midday smoke was signalled ahead, coming from a lone merchant vessel. The German officers could see her pitching and tossing; she seemed to be making no headway. The *Tirpitz* flashed a signal for her to stop and when she disregarded the order the 6-inch guns opened fire at 6,000 yards. Five minutes later the merchant vessel sank. The Germans thought that it might be a straggler from the convoy and they were correct: it was a Russian cargo boat which had developed engine trouble. But the convoy remained invisible and the further north the attacking force sailed, the foggier grew the horizon.

On board the *Tirpitz*, Vice-Admiral Otto Ciliax was anxious. The three destroyers had signalled in turn that they needed refuelling. This sailing at high speed—or rather the maximum speed they could maintain in this heavy weather—had emptied their tanks. Normally they could have refuelled at sea through pipes from the battleship, but the present heavy weather made this operation just as impossible as the catapulting of aircraft. Much against his will the Admiral dismissed the destroyers with orders to put in at the nearest Norwegian port.

Thus the *Tirpitz* was alone without reconnaissance or protection—alone, just as the *Graf Spee* and the *Bismarck* had been. Admiral Ciliax seems to have been unaware that the British covering force was operating in the same waters. But the very fact that his ocean-going mastodon was alone must have made him anxious. Historians maintain that he found it unreasonable to risk a capital ship like the *Tirpitz* in chasing a convoy of merchant ships.

Twilight of the 7th March melted into the same moaning darkness as the previous evening and the battleship pursued her lonely course all night and part of the following morning. Without finding anything, it had reached a point ten miles south of Bear Island (N.N.W. of North Cape) when Ciliax received from Admiral Raeder the signal he had presumably been hoping for: *Abandon operation.* He immediately put about.

The British Admiralty was aware that the *Tirpitz* had

put to sea, for aircraft of Coastal Command had sighted her. They knew that the target of the German battleship could only be PQ 12. The covering force, informed of this, put on full speed to cut it off, but their progress was hampered by the rising storm.

Nevertheless, C.-in-C. Home Fleet refused to give up hope. At dawn on the 9th March, fighters rose from *H.M.S. Victorious* in the teeth of a furious gale and less than an hour later sighted the *Tirpitz* making for the Norwegian coast. Directly their report was received, twelve torpedo-carrying Fairey Albacores took off from the *Victorious*. They arrived in sight of the German battleship and, losing height, dived on their target almost like gliding magpies while the flak from the *Tirpitz* burst furiously round them. They pressed home the engagement as best they could, but a storm-tossed aircraft dropping a torpedo at high speed into that liquid chaos was not the ideal condition for an attack. The *Tirpitz* took violent evasive action and none of the torpedoes found its mark.

With the gale steadily increasing in force, the aircraft had great difficulty in landing on the carrier on their return. To receive them the *Victorious* had to turn westward into the wind and thus away from the enemy. Doubtless it was impossible to launch a further flight of aircraft. In the meantime the *Tirpitz,* aware that her life was at stake, ploughed into the mountainous waves like a ram. Shaken and buffeted to her vitals, she threw up enormous plumes of spray from her bows each time they rose from the seething water. Luckily for her, the Norwegian coast was not far away, and she entered the first large fjord within reach: West Fjord, defended by the Narvik forces. This time the game had been a draw.

And what of the convoy? The PQ 12 got through without being attacked. At the height of the storm, hidden by the cold fog, skirting the ice floes, it got through, almost blind but invisible. And the QP 8 was just as lucky, for fog concealed it as far as Iceland.

These were the results of the following voyages: the PQ 13 lost four cargo vessels; PQ 14 one; PQ 15 two cargo vessels and a corvette; QP 11 a Russian cargo, but the 10,000-ton cruiser *H.M.S. Edinburgh* escorting this convoy was sunk. Badly damaged by two U-boats which launched their torpedoes simultaneously, then attacked by torpedo-carrying aircraft, she was despatched by a torpedo in an attack by German destroyers.

In the great subterranean hall of the Convoy Office at Liverpool, naval officers followed the passage of all these ships on an enormous map across which the W.R.N.S. moved little cardboard figures to show the ships' positions according to messages received.

The German officers could not follow with the same ease all the movements of the Allied convoys, but since Murmansk was only a few minutes' flight from the Norwegian airfields, no shipping movements near that port escaped their notice.

In this way the sailing of the QP was immediately reported. Admiral Raeder gave orders for destroyers and submarines to put to sea, and for aircraft to take off irrespective of the weather. The QP convoys were less interesting than those making for the Russian ports, since they carried no war material; but any ship sunk represented a victory in the struggle to destroy Allied tonnage. Furthermore, the vessels in the QP convoys did not always sail in ballast. They brought back from the U.S.S.R. chromium, potassium, magnesium, furs and eider-duck feathers.

Moreover, there was no ban on the aggressors attacking the escort vessels. Some of the merchant ships in PQ 16 (we shall deal with this convoy later) had already accomplished the two-way trip before the Germans put up any serious opposition.

On the preceding voyages, the seamen of PQ 16 had only the summary information I have already mentioned and which was often far from accurate. They merely knew for certain that the situation had deteriorated.

At the same period, the news of the American Admiral Wilcox being washed overboard in the Atlantic reached the British ports. This is how the accident happened.

In March, 1942, Great Britain, needing to divert a few large units to attack Madagascar, asked the United States to relieve—at least partially for three months—the naval force escorting the convoys in the Arctic. On the 25th March, Task Force 39 set sail from Casco Bay, near Portland, Maine, under the command of Rear-Admiral John W. Wilcox. His fleet was composed of the 35,000-ton battleships *Washington* and *North Carolina,* the 14,700-ton aircraft carrier *Wasp,* the heavy cruisers *Wichita* and *Tuscalousa* and the 8th destroyer flotilla.

The storm which had shaken the *Tirpitz* continued to rage all over the whole Atlantic. Hardly had they put to sea than the task force was in its grip. One can get some idea of its violence from the following detail: the flying deck of the *Wasp,* fifty-one feet above the water-line, was swept by the waves. On the 26th March at 42° 24′ N., 69° 34′ W., Admiral Wilcox was swept overboard from the *Washington.* He had come on deck in his boots and a sou'wester and was making for the ladder leading to the bridge. He was suddenly seen up to the thighs in the green water and being dragged to the side ; then he disappeared over the side. The battleship circled but no body could be seen in the huge rollers and there was no chance of lowering a boat. To set his mind at rest, the Captain of the *Washington* asked over the T.B.S. if the *Wasp* could send up an aircraft. She headed into the wind and a few moments later the plane was airborne. It was seen to leave the flying deck, rise, bank and come down to within a few feet of the water. Suddenly it seemed to side-slip ; it banked and hit the water, to sink immediately, almost in the exact spot where the Admiral had disappeared. The sea swallowed up everything and nothing came to the surface. No attempt at rescue was possible. The task force re-formed and sailed on its way. Aboard the *Washington,* Admiral Wilcox's pennant was lowered and the flag flown at half-mast. A few moments later the new Commander's pennant was hoisted in the cruiser *Wichita*: Rear-Admiral R. C. Giffen had taken over command.

On its arrival at Scapa Flow, Task Force 39, less the aircraft carrier *Wasp,* diverted to deliver aircraft to Malta, joined the following British units: the battleship *H.M.S. King George V;* the aircraft carrier *H.M.S. Victorious;* the heavy cruiser *H.M.S. Kenya* and five destroyers. This fleet was given the name of Task Force 99. It set sail on the 28th April from Scapa Flow to protect the voyages of PQ 15 and QP 11. As we have already seen it did not prevent the sinking of the cruiser *H.M.S. Edinburgh.* Its action on this occasion showed a loss. While the formation was sailing in a thick fog, the *King George V* cut the destroyer *H.M.S. Punjabi* in two.

The sailors in convoy PQ 16 naturally had no idea of the strength of this powerful task force cruising in the North Atlantic and the Arctic Ocean. They only knew from rumours that the convoy escorts were becoming more and more important ; this both reassured and disturbed them at the same time.

Among them were British and Americans, Norwegians, Dutch, Danes, Poles, Greeks, Yugo-Slavs, Turks, Canadians, New Zealanders, Australians, Panamanians, Costa Ricans, Hawaians and men of other nationalities and of dubious nationality.

A few of them were definitely servicemen ; for example, the ratings who manned the guns in the merchant ships. Some, like the crews of the British cargo vessels, were mobilised on board their ships or, to be more exact, " commissioned " and subjected to military or quasi-military discipline. Others, like the American merchant seamen, remained almost entirely civilians, and could, if their vessel remained three or four months in a Russian port, earn at least 3,000 dollars for each two-way Arctic trip. The conditions of the Mercantile Marine in wartime varies according to nationalities and sometimes within the framework of a single nationality. It would need a long chapter and perhaps an entire book to deal with this subject, and I wonder if an expert in international law could clearly define, for example, the position of a sailor of Turkish nationality serving in a Panamanian cargo vessel, freighted by an American company, when he found himself among the men of convoy PQ 16.

While waiting to sail, the crews of the convoy PQ 16 were not bound to remain aboard. Each day the little boats which plied in the roadstead landed them at Greenock or Gourock, from where most of them took the train to Glasgow. Here they slaked their thirst in the pubs outside St. Enoch's or Central Station, visiting several in turn for, since whisky was rationed, they could only get a certain amount in each one.

In due course, the night train was caught in order to be back on board early next morning. They slept at Greenock or Gourock in the Seamen's Rests, where they were taken in free. Those who arrived too late to find accommodation went to the police station. The Inspector telephoned to all the local inhabitants who had a room or a bed for the liberty men. All the neighbouring towns, both large and small, were over-populated, invaded by soldiers and sailors whom the civilians tried to lodge, to welcome and entertain. This solicitude much impressed the American sailors.

Early in the morning the small steamers drew alongside to take on the liberty men, some of them in a state of considerable hangover, for they were all only too aware of the demands that the next few days—perhaps weeks—would make of them.

On the 4th May, workmen from the British shipyards arrived to fit anti-aircraft machine-guns on the cargo boats

which were still unarmed. Two double 30 mm. Marlins
were mounted on the roof of the deck-house, one on each
quarter and two more to stern ; old American weapons
from 1918, painted khaki. The United States had made a
present of them to Great Britain to equip her aircraft and
they had now been modified for manual firing. After the
workmen, an old Royal Navy armourer arrived to deliver
a brief gunnery course, dismantling a gun and explaining
how it functioned to men who had never handled one
before.

" This can fire 700 rounds a minute," said the old
gunner. "Always remember to fire before Jerry does. Show
him the pretty pink colour of your tracers. He's not a
superman and he clings on to life just like you or I. If
he sees the fire coming too close he'll run for cover." He
showed excessive optimism, probably based on First World
War experience or perhaps he spoke in this way to reassure
those who were going on the Arctic run.

Nearly all the seamen listened to him attentively and
later practised handling the machine-gun, aiming at English machines flying over the roadstead. There were dis-
cussions in several of the American ships, for the sailors
asked why they had not fitted a real gun on board with
regular Navy gunners to man it. It wasn't their job, they
said, to learn how to fire a machine-gun. Others replied
that it probably wasn't their job, but the presence in the
holds of a few hundred pounds of T.N.T. should make
them understand that anything which could drive off an
aircraft was useful—even four antiquated machine-guns
—and that it wasn't a bad thing to learn how to use them.

The artillery on board the ships of PQ 16 was disparate.
It consisted of 20 mm and 30 mm machine-guns and
cannon of the following calibres: 37, 76, 88, 102, 126, 135
and 140 mm. These guns were manned either by merchant
seamen or by naval ratings. The latter were on good terms
with the crews, although this was more often the case on

board the British ships, for in the American cargo vessels and tankers relations were often strained or bad.

The personnel of the naval armed guards in the American ships was recruited mainly from young men who had never been to sea before. They had received their gunnery instruction just before they embarked. A few guards were commanded by old naval gunner officers who had retired and been recalled to the service, but most of them were under the orders of young reserve ensigns who were as raw as their men. The task of these young officers was extremely difficult and it is surprising that they were so often up to it. They had to train their little group and to maintain discipline in the disorderly atmosphere of a merchant ship. They had to remain on good terms with the crew so that they would agree to handle the ammunition and eventually to replace the regular ratings who had been killed or wounded. And finally they had to be on good terms with the Mercantile Marine officers who were inclined to look upon them as rookies and to indulge in a laugh if they saw them in difficulties. According to official reports, open hostility between the naval armed guards and the crews reigned at the outset in thirty per cent. of the American ships.

Waterproof life-saving suits were distributed to those who did not yet possess them. This standard equipment, invented by a civilian official of the Ministry of War Transport, consisted of a pair of ordinary seaboots and a bright orange one-piece rubber suit of the same thickness and the same texture as a good mackintosh. Beneath this garment, which served as a protection from both heat and cold, the sailor wore his ordinary clothes plus a light life-jacket. The wrists were well fitted, the garment was tightened at the collar by a double cord and completed by a hood, also bright orange. The whole kit weighed only three pounds and could be carried in a pack like a gasmask. At sea the men were told to keep it out of the pack, carefully folded so that they could grab it and put it on quickly. At night it was placed, folded up, on their shoes, next to their bunk.

The recipients of this gift were in a hurry to examine all the seams, to put it on and try it. They found it comfortable but rather too clinging for swimming. They realised that they might have to wear it for days on end during uninterrupted attacks, half-asphyxiated and exhausted by this waterproof, knowing that if they took it off the first dive into the icy water would prove fatal.

On the 9th May, which was a Saturday, week-end leave was granted and the sailors took advantage of this to go to Edinburgh, two hours away by train. The merchant seamen in Princes Street saw a great military parade with men from all the Services wearing superb uniforms: Royal Army Service Corps, confident Commandos, Scots with their hackles and kilts, Indians in shorts and turbans, Free Norwegians, Free French and Free Poles, men of the Royal Navy and even a delegation from British Merchant Navy, men in caps without braid and blue double-breasted jackets, carrying the red duster with the union jack in the corner. This participation of the British Merchant Navy in the military parade was a new cause for comment, comparison and reflection for the men of the American vessels, providing a rich topic of conversation in the pubs and bars.

Edinburgh is a magnificent old granite city. At night the black-out completely restored it to its ancient majesty, with the castle keep standing out black against a starry sky. Everywhere in the dark streets rang the clatter of hobnailed boots and little blue stars arose from the pavement. None of the boys on leave ever forgot this detail. They all slept at the Servicemen's Home and the following afternoon a certain number of them attended the big military concert in Princes Street Gardens. The First Brigade of Polish Fusiliers and the bagpipes of the Royal Scots played in turn. The men lay on the grass, sitting among clusters of yellow crocuses as the sun shone in a blue sky and the mild air showed that spring was at hand. Children ran about and women in neat suits were walking with the officers. Leaning on their elbows among the crocuses, chewing blades of grass, the men remained for a moment silent, enjoying this vision of spring, of the burgeoning of life despite the war. How many of them would live to see the summer?

CHAPTER TWO

Outward Bound

FROM THE 11TH MAY ONWARDS THE MER-
chant ships began to leave Greenock roads. Not in convoys
but in very small groups or even on their own, following
the pilots who took them down the Firth of Clyde as far
as the North Channel and then along the coast in a
northerly direction.

The Scottish coast seen from close quarters affords a
spectacle unique in beauty. The crews saw mauve mountains raising their heads above the early morning mist
which the sun soon dispersed. The highlands appeared
brown and grey and then the green slopes fell sheer into
the calm waters of the loch. This pleasure trip lasted
twenty-four hours. At the end of it, behind a reddish promontory, the sailors discovered the vessels which had sailed
before them and a few dark silhouettes of warships. The
name of this convoy assembly place has become historical:
Loch Ewe.

Hardly had they anchored than naval barges came alongside and R.N. ratings began to load the ammunition boxes.
The merchant ships also received some additional apparatus such as boxes of smoke floats and flares. The PAC flares
could fire two small parachutes joined together by 160
yards of piano wire, designed to break the propellers of the
aircraft. This ingenious gadget does not seem to have been
very effective. I have never heard mention of any aircraft
brought down by it.

On the evening of the 14th of May the captains of all
the merchant vessels were summoned to a conference by

the Commodore, and on the morning of the 15th the convoy set sail for Iceland.

The first convoys to become famous in history were the Gold Fleets of the sixteenth century, which carried the riches of the New World back to Spain. It is easy to realize that this type of navigation demands special discipline. Without it one merely gets a dangerous mob, impossible to defend effectively, and an enormous and vulnerable target.

The convoy was under the orders of a Commodore who flew his flag in one of the merchant ships. He took all the decisions with regard to navigation and the defensive action of his fleet. He prescribed the zig zags, changes of course and, if necessary, changes of itinerary in order to avoid an enemy that had been reported. He saw that the security measures were observed, that the boat showed the least smoke possible by day and no lights by night. He kept in touch with the senior officer of the escort and operated in collaboration with him. He wielded complete command over all the ships in the convoy like an admiral of olden days. His responsibility was sometimes heavier and more urgent than that of many modern admirals. But the fleet under his command was formed of merchant ships of all sizes, some trim, some unwieldy, commanded by a great variety of captains, some of whom were convinced that whatever he did his orders were designed solely to exasperate if not harm them. The Higher Authorities had long been aware of this state of affairs and this is why the duties of Commodore (the term defines a duty and not a rank) were generally carried out by old sea dogs chosen for their experience, authority and reputation. They were retired admirals and other senior officers of the R.N. or old merchant skippers, of fifty to sixty-five and more. During the Second World War, a sixty-eight-year-old Commodore commanded several convoys until ill-health and exhaustion forced him to remain ashore. The Commodore was at sea on an average 150 days of the year during which he hardly ever undressed, lying down for a few hours at night on a camp bed in the chart-house. We shall see that this precarious rest was rarely allowed the Commodores in Arctic waters. During the Second World War about thirty of the Commodores went down with their ships.

The night before they sailed, the Commodore convened the captains. He told them the composition of the convoy and its formation, *i.e.* the number of columns (from four to six or eight to ten) and the place of each boat represented by a number. He also informed them of their destination, the route or successive routes and the speed. He gave them the signal code to be used during the crossing, the written instructions concerning transmissions and those indicating the method of sailing in zig-zags at a given signal. The object of the conference was to provide these captains with such complete and precise instructions that once the convoy was at sea the exchange of messages could be limited to absolutely unavoidable cases. For this reason the Commodore also told them, not only the destination but the successive rallying points in case of dispersal. He appointed a Vice-Commodore who would take over command in case he was sunk and a Rear-Commodore to replace him in case of need. Finally, he informed them of all the zones reputed dangerous according to the latest reports and gave them the last weather forecasts.

According to his temperament and the reactions of his audience, he added or omitted a few personal words of exhortation, advice and encouragement.

The skippers listened and asked questions. Some of them showed intelligence, professional competence and goodwill. Others raised meaningless, too often voiced objections and he had to reply to them with the greatest tact. As a general rule his authority took the upper hand—at least for a time—and the conference broke up in an atmosphere of cordiality.

The convoy began to form as soon as the ships had crossed the anti-submarine net which barred the entrance to the loch. Each ship flew the flag with its number and did its best to take up its place swiftly in the procession. The weather was fine and the sea calm. No escort vessels had yet appeared. The aircraft of Coastal Command flew above the convoy ; they were Sunderland flying boats or Catalinas, giant seaplanes, slow and extremely vulnerable in aerial combat but excellent for detecting and attacking submarines. Naturally these R.A.F. escorts did not remain like balloons above the convoy. However slow they may have been, their speed was still fifteen to twenty times faster than that of the ships. They patrolled round the formation and particularly ahead of it, but they often returned to show themselves to the crews in order to give them confidence.

From the low altitude at which they flew, the airmen could distinguish on the decks serried lines of vehicles like brand-new toys ; planes covered with bright transparent tarpaulins, army lorries, petrol trucks and tanks. The convoy consisted of twenty-five boats of different tonnage sailing in six columns. From the air they seemed to be stationary, following in the wake of the other and almost deserted. They could see no men, only an occasional tiny dot here and there. Sometimes they had to look very attentively to see if they were really moving.

The sailors, too, had no real picture of their convoy. Contrary to what one might imagine, sailing in convoy does not give the impression of a great human gathering. The ships were 900 yards apart. From each of them their shipmates in the other ships were only visible as little impersonal shapes, small robots whom they could occasionally see, motionless on the bridges. These travelling companions remained as unknown as if they had not seen them at all.

On the other hand, the ships themselves rapidly acquired a personality even to a landlubber. After less than a day at sea one could recognise at first sight a certain number merely by the way she rose gently on the swell or fell into the trough, or by the way her funnel smoked, or because she kept slightly ahead or astern of her position. In this way the ship became a sort of living being whereas the men disappeared.

Toward midday, two destroyers and two corvettes caught up the convoy and took up their positions ahead and on either side. The seaplanes of Coastal Command flew off to the south.

The uninitiated often ask what sailors do during uneventful days. It is very simple. When they are not on duty they do as they please, that is to say, they sleep, play cards or make and mend. Some of them read old dog-eared magazines, the Bible if they are devout. When on watch, of course, they each have their own duty: the engineers and stokers below, the deck hands at the helm, the voice pipes, the signals, on look out for aircraft and submarines or at ordinary duty such as washing and painting. In principle, each man is on duty eight hours a day. In the British and American cargo vessels the day is divided into watches in the following manner: midnight to four, four to eight, eight to twelve midday and twelve to four. Then come the dog-watches, to break the succession so that each man shall have a different watch each day. Four to six and six to eight, etc., etc.

In the morning and at midday or when the sun deigned to appear, the captain or one of his junior officers took a bearing with the sextant to calculate the position. At nightfall the Commodore signalled his orders for the night if there were any changes from the original orders. This was also the hour for admonishments: " No. 12, make less smoke. No. 19, keep your position better."

The means of communication within the convoy were as follows: megaphones, flags, Aldis lamp, coloured flares, sirens, telegraphy and telephony (T.B.S.). The most rapid and most convenient method was the T.B.S., transmitted on very short waves with a range of not more than thirty miles, inaudible to submarines when submerged. Signals were sent in clear by using a code to design the ships' numbers, the routes and the hours. But the Authorities constantly discouraged the use of radio in the convoy for the enemy aircraft could pick it up. At night the only means authorised were the siren and the megaphone.

In all the ships the wireless operators were constantly listening for messages from the land reporting dangers, the met., and any news that might be useful. These messages were sent on powerful long waves with low frequency. The land stations sent messages one after the other several times a day in Morse at slow speed (eighteen words a minute) to allow reception by the least experienced operators. The text was in code, changing each day.

The reception of these messages was easy, but the deciphering was often a nightmare, not only for the merchant navy officers. In bad weather in the damp " cabouches " of destroyers and corvettes, the wireless operators, sometimes in their waterproof suits, engaged in a real physical combat with their code books and pads which refused to stay on the table, fell on the damp lino or into the sea.

The messages convoy - Admiralty were sent only by the Commodores and escort leaders and reduced to a minimum. Each day about midday the Commodore sent the position of the convoy in a brief coded message with no apparent indication of the addressee.

On the morning of the 18th May, the men of PQ 16 saw Coastal Command aircraft based on Iceland arriving from the North. The Icelandic coast appeared that morning: a flat drab shore with a background of snowy mountains, the tall, massive one being the volcano Hekla. A little later grass and vegetation could be seen on the slopes and foreshore. The convoy began to make its way along the coast. The crews could see a few unimportant villages with pretty modern houses. Some of the men had already landed in Iceland and the others asked them questions. What are the people like? Do they speak English? Are they hospitable? It must be terribly cold up here in the winter, eh? And they received the following replies: " The Icelanders are very like the Norwegians. Most of the young ones speak English. The temperature is not particularly low in winter but there is usually a biting cold wind blowing. The houses are comfortable and everything is very modern but the reception is rather frigid. They don't like us."

The convoy anchored in a deep fjord where they found several other cargo vessels, large tankers and warships. In the distance they could see the harbour and the town of Reykjavik. The houses were nearly all gleaming white with black, red, pink or pale green roofs. Here and there a few long khaki Nissen huts. . . . No trees. . . . Through their glasses they could see jeeps driving at full speed, small shaggy ponies, Icelanders and children dressed in colours as bright as the roofs. It was exciting enough to arouse curiosity despite the disillusioned remarks of those who had already been there. But the rumour soon ran round that they would not be allowed ashore.

Seals swam in the water round the boats ; they sported, dived and surfaced with fantastic grace, staring with bold eyes at the sailors watching them from the deck.

It was nearly 9 o'clock before the sun disappeared below the horizon and there was not much more than an hour of real darkness. The long twilight returned and the sun rose over black snow and ice-capped mountains streaked by huge waterfalls. A fine plume of mist lay like a wreath on the summit of Hekla. The men regarded this natural beauty with a jaundiced eye. They were tired of being chivvied from pillar to post ; since they could not go ashore they might just as well leave as soon as possible.

On the 19th May and the night of the 19th/20th visits were exchanged between ships. The captains invited each other abroad, taking their officers and men with them. Whisky flowed in abundance, shouts, songs and even revolver shots disturbed the peace of the fjord. Many of the American skippers were loth to abandon the tradition that " the master of the ship after God " should never be without his revolver. On the way back to their ships they fired at empty boxes floating on the water, at seals or anything they saw. Luckily there were no accidents.

A very much visited boat that night was the *Starye Bolchevik,* the Russian vessel in the convoy. The men who had visited the Soviet Union were filled with curiosity. They found a clean ship-shape vessel. The Captain offered them sweet tea with white bread and butter. The *Starye Bolchevik* had a gun-crew provided by the Royal Navy on board. An unusual phenomenon was the presence of women among the crew. One of these, a young rather fragile-looking girl, was the second engineer's wife. The other two, pretty blondes, were stewardesses.

Convoy PQ 16 sailed from Reykjavik on the 20th May at 20.00. At full complement it comprised thirty-four cargo vessels and tankers of varying tonnage, some more than twenty years old, others brand new like the Liberty ships. One of the cargo boats, the *Alynbank* of about 8,000 B.R.T., was armed with a powerful ack-ack and equipped with radar. Another was a cam-ship, *i.e.* it carried an aircraft and a catapult.

The escort was made up of the following units (three or four of the less important sailing from Seydhisfjordhur would not join them until the early hours of the 22nd, but are included in the total): the cruisers H.M.S. *Nigeria, Liverpool, Kent* and *Norfolk*; six destroyers; four corvettes; six armed sloops; two flak-ships (auxiliary cruisers); two submarines and a naval tanker (to refuel the destroyers and corvettes).

To these must be added a rescue ship whose captain and crew were merchant seamen, all volunteers; she carried a surgeon and sick bay attendants provided by the Royal Navy. The rescue ships were small cargo vessels of 1,500 tons, formerly coasters in the North Sea and the Irish Channel. They hurried to the scene of any sinking to pick up the survivors. (The remaining vessels in the convoy were not allowed to stop or manoeuvre to pick up survivors; they would risk being sunk themselves and any break in the convoy would have made it more vulnerable. The escorts picked up as many as they could but only after they had repelled the attackers.) When the rescue ships were in action at night they used their lights and even their searchlights. They were unarmed, but were not protected by international convention like the hospital ships. The enemy did not usually attack them. On one occasion, however, one of them was deliberately torpedoed and sunk.

The convoy proceeded for about thirty hours along the coast rounding the north-west of Iceland. To starboard the men saw the sombre fjords and dark mountains half covered with snow. But soon they had no time to watch the shore, for the ships received orders to drop their fog buoys. These consisted of a towline at the end of which was a piece of wood with a copper hood; it raised a very visible wake three to five feet high so that each ship could easily follow his "leader" and keep his place in the column. The escort vessels kept their positions by sound or by their radar.

The fog grew denser. It clung to the face and entered the lungs. For each ship his neighbours became pale wraiths until they disappeared completely, swallowed up in this icy cotton wool. At regular intervals the ships sounded their foghorns.

The *Alcoa Banner* lost the convoy about midday on the 23rd May. The lookout men had sighted an iceberg and the Captain had to change course to avoid it.

The iceberg had appeared a hundred yards dead ahead; a strange electric blue in the fog; it was about thirty feet high and as large as a small house. The Captain gave the

order: " Hard to starboard," and the crew saw the iceberg
float past on the other bow shrouded, as they put it, in a
definitely perceptible cold zone. The Captain then tried
to take up his position again, but the fog buoy of the
preceding vessel had disappeared and no wake was visible
in the small area of discoloured sea ahead. Perhaps the
leading ship also had to avoid the iceberg.

The Captain of the *Alcoa Banner* altered course slightly
to port in the direction of the foghorns and put on speed.
He dared not cut obliquely across the convoy for fear of a
collision. The present course should have brought him back
to the starboard column, and yet the foghorn blasts grew
more muffled. In the heart of the fog nothing ever happens
logically or even credibly.

At 15.00 it became obvious that they had lost the convoy.
The Captain could only navigate by dead reckoning and
try to reach the rallying point arranged for the following
midday. This was a reasonable hope for the fog was now
lifting. But the end of the fog would almost certainly mean
intervention on the part of the enemy. The chance of a
solitary cargo vessel in these waters was exceedingly slight.

About 16.00 the fog grew considerably less dense. The
lookouts scanned the sea and the white half globe that
spread round the ship. Suddenly they heard the throb
of a ship's engine and saw white foam at the bows of a long
thin shape. In a few seconds the craft drew alongside. It
was a British destroyer flying the White Ensign.

All the gunners were at action stations on her deck. She
gave the impression of energy, efficiency and watchfulness.
Some of the crew stared in silence at the *Alcoa Banner*,
others kept looking up at the sky where the sun seemed to
be breaking through. The destroyer was now sailing at the
same speed as the cargo vessel. On the small bridge they
could see two officers with red smiling faces in duffle coats
and cap. One of them, obviously the Captain, called over
the loud hailer: " What ship, please? "

The amplification was stupendous, quite out of proportion to his small stature. It sounded as though the destroyer herself was speaking. The skipper of the *Alcoa Banner* took his megaphone and gave the name of his ship.

" Your number, please? "

" No. 13." The officers of the destroyer burst out laughing.

" Ha, Ha! You've got a lucky number, eh? But you'd better get back to the fold as soon as possible. We're expecting air and submarine attacks. Here is your course and sail at full speed. We're remaining with you."

Several other cargoes who had stayed in the fog were found and brought back to the convoy by the destroyer escort on the 23rd and 24th May. On the 24th about 16.00 one of the cruisers hoisted a black flag to show that a submarine had been detected. Two destroyers streaked at full speed south and then east dropping their depth charges. The engineers and stokers of the merchant ships could hear their explosions quite distinctly. But there was no attack that day.

The following day the fog lifted at about 06.00. A quarter of an hour later a Dornier 18 was observed for a few minutes flying at a great height above the clouds. It disappeared. At 08.00 the convoy reached Long.3°12′E., Lat.70°14′N. Beyond this latitude the sun never sets. At 13.00 a second suspicious aircraft was seen out of range to the south. The weather cleared even more and the temperature fell considerably. The calm sea was dotted with a host of small icebergs. At 18.25 the *Alynbank* sent a signal: "Aircraft 17 miles south approaching the convoy." The crews went to their action stations in all the ships.

CHAPTER THREE

The Voyage of PQ 16

THE *City of Joliet*, ONE OF THE VESSELS
in convoy PQ 16, was a 10,000-ton Liberty ship with an
overall length of 415 feet and 51 feet at the waist. She had
two decks, four holds (net tonnage 4,380 tons), two Diesel
engines, an auxiliary engine developing 2,500 hp, and a
four-bladed screw; her average speed was eleven knots
giving her a range of 17,000 miles. She was brand new
and this was her maiden voyage. As is well known, the
Liberty ships were mass produced. They were built to
last five years.

Her crew consisted of thirty-nine seamen plus twelve
naval armed guards commanded by an ensign from the
Reserve. None of these ratings or the merchant seamen
had ever been in a real air attack. One of them, Davis
Doyle, had been twice shipwrecked, but both times as the
result of a torpedo attack. The tragedy had been almost
instantaneous: a violent shock that made the ship shudder,
bits of iron and wood flying through the air, a column
of steam as the boiler groaned like a huge wounded beast.
Both sinkings had been similar down to the smallest
details. Davis remembered that he had hardly had time
to be scared.

On the 24th May, 1942, about 18.30, the sailors manning
the 20 mm Oerlikon on the upper bridge noticed at Green
75° ahead four aircraft skimming the waves followed by
six others which were gaining height. They were painted
silver and gleamed in the sun. Those flying at wave-top
level—about 50 feet—were torpedo-carrying Heinkel 115s.
They were now nearer than the other flight.

The escort vessel had been firing at them for some time and soon all the guns and machine guns were in action. The din was incredible but occasionally in a lull certain tones could be heard: the 140s, 135s and even the 102s gave their deep cannon note, dull and vibrant ; they were accompanied by the rapid staccato barking of the 37s and the clatter of the machine guns. As the aircraft approached the noise became more intense and uninterrupted. The tracers were rose-pink, scarlet or even khaki-coloured.

The Heinkels launched their torpedoes at about a mile from the outside starboard column. (In actual fact the torpedo bomber does not launch its torpedo but releases it like an ordinary bomb. The mechanism which releases the projectile at the same time starts the engine which propels this little ship at a speed of thirty-six knots. Each Heinkel carries two torpedoes twenty-one feet in length with a diameter of 533 mm and weighing about a ton.)

The crew of The City of Joliet saw the release of the torpedoes. The aircraft suddenly raised its nose, flattened out and climbed like a dive bomber after it had launched; but the " flattening-out " and all the movements are different from those of the dive bomber. The crew of the merchant ship could clearly distinguish the splash of white foam when the torpedoes hit the sea. Then they saw the tracks which seemed like a long white scar spreading out at full speed ; as it drew closer the bubbles were visible.

The sailors counted four tracks: two followed by a second pair. They realised at once that these torpedoes had not been aimed at their ship, the tracks were too far to stern. In that direction a ship in the line was already veering to starboard. Two destroyers sped towards the aircraft, at the same time firing grenades with percussion fuses to explode the torpedoes or divert their course. Other vessels of the starboard centre columns (the convoy sailed in five parallel columns) were also taking avoiding action. No ship was hit.

The Heinkels had circled and were in position to attack

once more. They launched their torpedoes almost from the same distance. Several ships began to scurry in all directions like sheep chased by a dog ; the destroyers at full speed, with great white moustaches on either side of the bows, shot off their fireworks, leaving huge geysers of water from their direct action grenades in their wake. No ship was hit.

The six aircraft following the Heinkels but gaining height were Junkers 88 dive-bombers. They arrived in line abreast 300 yards apart and after climbing to about 7,500 feet broke formation and dived individually on their targets.

In the bowels of *The City of Joliet* reigned the rhythmic hum of the auxiliary engine, distinguishable from all the other noises—almost like the beating of a human heart. The Liberty ships were equipped with auxiliary engines in preference to turbines on account of the simple and robust character and also because spare parts and engineers who could service them could be found in any harbour in the world.

The greaser Charles C. Coleman, " Shorty " to his ship-mates, listened to this rhythmic breathing and at the same time to the pounding of his own heart. He wondered if once more the shudders would run through the ship and he would have the courage to bear them ; he must control his mad urge to shin up the iron companion ladder on to the deck and run to one of the boats.

The shudders that " Shorty " had just felt were the explosions of the " hedgehogs " fired by the destroyers ; but no one in the engine room could have known that. The men on deck had already donned their life-saving suits and were ready for any eventuality. But one could not work below in such a garment. Shorty said to himself that it was terrible he did not even have his life-jacket near to hand. It hung with some others on a rack in the boiler room. He should have had it with him. But to work in these conditions would have been impossible.

Shorty was only a poor wretch who by rights should not

have clung on to life. He was an orphan. He had memories of a shabbily dressed man and woman walking through the streets playing a harmonium and singing hymns while he sang with them ; but he knew that this man and woman were not his parents ; he was only a waif who had been brought up in an institution. After a rather drab though varied existence, he had embarked at the age of seventeen as a boy greaser in one of the Great Lakes steamers. In May, 1942, he was 27 and a professional sailor and still a greaser. He told himself that he must have been crazy to have carried his kit aboard one of these cargoes destined for the Arctic. He had done so merely because he had been tired of staying ashore even before his last leave had expired.

At the moment, Shorty was standing in the after-end of the engine room, a huge oil can with a broad lip in his right hand ; a rag round his left hand. He tightened the rivet of this implement, or rather pretended to do so, looking in the direction of the office. Near it were the Third Engineer and an apprentice standing by the phone looking very scared. To starboard, two men were busy mending a feed pump. They were silent and seemed to be working very leisurely. Perhaps they too were frightened. Dogby, the old stoker, was somewhere out of sight in the boiler room ; he also was probably scared . . . As for the Third Engineer, Shorty could only see his back ; he was examining the gauges with his hand on the wheel of a valve.

All these men were at their posts. From where they stood they could all reach the iron ladder in a flash. If the worst happened they could drop everything and make for the ladder. It would not be so easy for Shorty. He decided that he could not stay where he was much longer, pretending to tighten the rivet. It was now time to go and grease the plummer blocks of the shaft. To do this he had to walk to the end of the engine room, cross the after hatch and make his way along the tunnel containing the long powerful steel rod with the screw at the end. The moment had

45

come to grease the blocks. The idea of going along this tunnel now terrified him. He had to bend down and it was a difficult task. The man who was caught there at the moment of a catastrophe would certainly have no chance of getting out.

The bridge phone rang. The engineer's mate took the message and began to talk in a tense voice to his superior.

A terrible shudder ran through the engine room. Not only this compartment but the whole ship vibrated as though The City of Joliet had been transformed into an enormous bell. At the second shudder the floor listed. The vessel was obviously taking avoiding action. At least it was to be hoped that this was the reason for the list.

Shorty began to walk—he was almost staggering—not to the rear of the compartment but in the direction of the ladder. At the last moment he made his way towards the office. He came up behind the Third Engineer, who turned round.

" What's wrong?" he asked.

Shorty opened his mouth to speak but could not utter a word. His heart was beating furiously. He glanced at the boy, who immediately lowered his eyes. Over the boy's shoulder he caught sight of the port oil pump.

"The oil pump's blocked," he said, looking at the officer again.

It was true. The vibration had ceased. The Third Engineer looked in its direction.

" Oh, yes. Thanks."

He turned round and ordered the two men who were working on the feed pumps to get the oil pump started again. Then he turned once more to Shorty and repeated " Thanks." He glanced up at the top of the iron ladder down which appeared a pair of short blue legs which could only belong to the Chief. Shorty followed his gaze.

A third tremor ran through the ship. This time the floor plating seemed to rise. Each man had clutched on to something. The Chief clung to the ladder and when

46

the ship righted herself continued to descend. At last Shorty left the office and began to walk aft, towards the tunnel. There was nothing else he could do. No, he could not have acted differently.

Later, Shorty explained all these details to the reporters who questioned him in his adventures. He described his life in the engine room during the attacks without trying to hide the fact that he was terrified. No, it was not patriotism which forced him to carry on with his job in spite of everything ; he did not give it a thought ; nor a wish to preserve his self-respect. It was far more a feeling of resignation, the idea that he could not do anything else . . .

Shorty entered the tunnel and began to grease the blocks. More tremors ran through the ship. Bent double and with death in his soul, full of self-pity that wrung the tears from his eyes, he had a mad urge to leave the tunnel, to rush for the ladder and to climb it at top speed. But he did nothing.

The vessel was shaken and buffeted several times. She was weaving to escape the bombs. But these violent shocks began to twist and buckle the hull plates.

Five ships were hit by bombs in the course of this attack. Hardly had the target been hit than smoke rose. Now most of the merchant ships were carrying a few hundred pounds of T.N.T. From the deck of *The City of Joliet,* the men watched these columns of smoke expecting the explosions from one moment to the next. But nothing of the kind happened. The fires were got under control. The convoy sailed on in full complement.

There was one comic interlude. At the height of the action, when every ship was defending itself as best it could against the dive bombers, a signal was flown by H.M.S. *Nigeria,* the escort leader. The men on the bridge rushed for their binoculars and the officers consulted the code book. The signal read: " Put your watches forward one hour."

At 20.10 all the enemy aircraft had left. Nevertheless

a Blohm Voss 138 reconnaissance plane continued to circle above the enemy, well out of range of the guns. This "spotter" was to accompany them all the way to Murmansk. It was not always the same machine, of course, and its brother came to relieve it. But the crews felt that it was always the same hawk constantly circling in the sky. Several of the convoys were accompanied in this way throughout their journey. Since there was no night, the hawk never lost sight of the convoy. The wireless operators heard him sending messages. He kept calling U-boats and aircraft like a mother hen calling her chicks. Apart from the danger from this constant observation, the presence of the hawk was exasperating. Legend has it that a certain Commodore sent a message to the pilot one day: "You're making me giddy, always flying round on the same tack." The hawk replied: "Sorry. Anything to oblige," and began to circle on the opposite tack.

At 21.00 the buzzers rang for action stations once more. The men who had shed their waterproof suits put them on again. The sky was clear as on a fine January afternoon in our latitudes. It was exceedingly cold—a dry cold.

At 21.10, twelve Ju 88s came out of the bright sun on the port quarter. This time the gunners were hampered by the dazzling light. They found it difficult to get these black mosquitoes which were moving fast against the shimmering background in their sights.

The City of Joliet's rear gun crew kept firing at one machine after the other. At 21.16 they realised that one of the Junkers was diving on them. The German plane began its dive at 7,500 feet; at that altitude it was impossible to determine its objective. But a few seconds later it was only too painfully obvious.

It is easy to put oneself in the shoes of those gunners in The City of Joliet. They were all very young tough fellows, in certain respects almost children. They had not had time to put on their waterproof suits when the attack started. They were wearing old dark blue reefers and

48

trousers of the same colour, tight at the ankles ; plimsolls, mittens and balaclavas. The gun layer was sitting on the right of the gun, his eye glued to the sights ; on the other side were the loader and a telegraphist. The rest of the crew relayed the long shells which they took from the ammunition chests.

The aircraft dived at about 50°. The sound of its engines which had started as a loud increasing drone developed into an eerie screech. To the gunners it seemed to be travelling much slower than the practice aircraft which had dived on them during their training period. Actually it was no slower, but the psychological premises were different.

The Junkers increased in size. This was noticeable by a thickening of its wings. Now they could distinguish the greenish yellow flames spurting from its cannon. All of them admitted that their most vivid impression was when they could distinctly see the bombs in their cradles—four large bombs. " It was extraordinary to be able to see those objects which within a few seconds might perhaps blow us to smithereens." The Junkers' cannon shells riddled the deck as they exploded but the men paid little heed to them. They represented little or no danger. Their whole fear was concentrated on those very visible bombs. (They did not cease firing despite the cannon fire and the sight of the bombs.)

Suddenly the German dropped one of his " eggs." (The Junkers could carry four 250-pound bombs.) The men saw it in the air; it seemed to float like a balloon while the plane pulled out of its dive and zoomed overhead with a thunderous roar. They saw the cylindrical shape of the khaki-coloured bomb. They could even see its vanes painted the same drab colour and the white serial numbers. All of them thought: " This is our number." As novices to aerial attack they did not know that the bomb which is destined for you always appears at a certain moment in the shape of a disc and then does not alter. So the men thought:

" It's for us," and at the same time they remembered the T.N.T. in the holds.

The bomb fell in the sea twenty yards to stern. A column of water rose in the air and the ship received a battering ram thrust which made her shudder. The empty shell cases lying on the deck were scattered in all directions. *The City of Joliet* danced on the waves as though a giant's invisible hand had picked her up and shaken her.

This bomb had been a near miss. By taking avoiding action the ship avoided many others between 21.00 and 22.00 on that 25th May. But the near explosions had damaged several more of her hull plates. She was now shipping water.

As in the preceding attack, several ships in the convoy were more or less seriously hit, but none of them sank. One however had to put back to Iceland and a tug was sent from Reykjavik to take her in tow. The convoy had left the Iceland capital five days before and had now completed about half its journey. The Commodore ordered the ship back because the remaining half was reputed to be far more difficult.

The first U-boat attack on the convoy took place on the 26th May, shortly after one o'clock in the morning.

We must not lose sight of the fact that the succession of dates here is only a convention which bears no resemblance to the reality lived by the sailors. For them there was one endless day without beginning or end, with the sun always in the sky, unless it was hidden by the fog; and events transpired against the background of this exhausting continuity. It is difficult to describe how painful the absence of darkness can be. All the accounts of sailors who have sailed the Arctic Ocean are unanimous on this point.

So, on the 26th May at one o'clock in the morning, the alarm bells sounded the submarine alert in all the ships of the convoy. There were no aircraft in the sky apart from the Blohm-Voss 138, which was still circling out of range.

The men at action stations on deck and the bridge of *The City of Joliet* saw several destroyers making at full speed towards the two escorting British submarines which were sailing on the surface. For some strange reason the cruisers were firing in the same direction.

The two British submarines separated, one to starboard and the other to port, and suddenly their movements revealed the target. Just between them a white or very light grey conning tower was clearly visible on the grey water. They could even see its diminutive wake. The British submarines machine-gunned it, but soon ceased their fire for fear of hitting the other vessels.

The crew of *The City of Joliet* saw only the grey conning tower for less than a minute. It had already crash-dived when the destroyers arrived, machine-gunning and firing depth charges. A mêlée ensued and it looked as though the destroyers and the two submarines were firing at each other and about to ram. Then all firing ceased and nothing remained except the explosions and the large waterspouts from the depth charges. The U-boat had completely disappeared. On board *The City of Joliet*, the men argued eagerly, some insisting that they had seen shells explode on the conning tower, others swearing that it had not been hit.

The controversy ended in speechlessness. On the starboard beam a column of fire spurted skywards. The cargo vessel *Syros*, loaded with explosives, had just been hit by a torpedo.

A column of blinding flame rose to 9,000 feet (the flames from these explosions of merchant ships crammed with explosives have never been accurately measured, but the estimation of naval officers is almost unanimous). A deafening roar, a suffocating displacement of air and a searing wind on the face . . . The pillar of fire grew larger, became a gigantic egg and changed colour. From a blinding white it turned carmine, scarlet and yellow. Then nothing. Not even a wisp of smoke against the pale blue sky. Nothing on the surface of the sea where five seconds before there had been a ship. No hulk, no floating wreckage. Each of the horrified spectators still had, in his eye so to speak, the precise outline of this ship which had existed there five seconds earlier: now there was nothing but the watery waste. This sudden absence seemed even more impressive than the column of fire.

It was all over. Of the fifty men in the *Syros* all that remained were names written in the shipping registers in heaven knows what ports, and a few photographs, a few clothes at home for those who had families. The same thing probably holds true of all those who died at sea. But the instantaneous annihilation of the sailors in the *Syros*, their total disintegration, had a most dramatic effect on the eye-witnesses. " It was terrible," said the crew of *The City of Joliet*. " It was as though they had never existed." And others said: " It was horrible ; one could hardly believe it was true."

About an hour after the *Syros* blew up, the four escorting cruisers left the convoy on a south-south-westerly course. The men in the cargo vessels watched them go and felt disappointed and nervous as they saw them disappear over the horizon.

The cruisers had possibly gone to meet an enemy surface force. This was the opinion held in most of the ships, including the other escort vessels ; but in certain documents we find: " It was too dangerous to expose warships larger than destroyers to air attacks from the land."

The merchandise carried by the convoys were useful and even precious and it was therefore necessary to protect them, but to know just how far this protection justified the exposure of warships far more precious than cargoes, was a delicate question. The premises constantly varied. It would be untrue to say that the risks run by the merchant seamen were never taken into account, but it is true that they counted for very little.

The convoy PQ 16 was now approaching the most dangerous part of the journey.

The men constantly scanned the sky to the south, in other words to starboard. The attackers could only come from there. Sometimes they attacked from astern or from the port beam but they always flew in from starboard. To port of PQ 16 stretched the polar ice. The sailors in the port column often saw huge ice fields quite close to them.

The men reckoned that in less than four days they would reach Murmansk, and before then the zone where the Russian fighters could protect the convoy. They forced themselves to think of this. They measured the time by the hours as they passed, and sometimes in quarter hours. Every moment that passed was a victory which brought them closer to their goal. No ship had been sunk since the torpedoing of the *Syros*. After all, the PQ 15 had only lost two ships.

But at 11.10 the enemy planes appeared. A moment later the destroyers' 4-inchers went into action and all the other ships followed suit.

From this first attack the crews realised the consequence of the cruisers having left. The diminution of the escort's fire power was hardly perceptible for the individual men, deafened by the guns of their own ships; but they all noticed that the bombers dived with far more audacity. Now they released their bombs at less than 300 feet. Several attacks took place that day between 11.10 and 23.00, with lulls of about two hours. Each time there were a few agonising moments when the bombers arrived over the convoy and broke formation. They could be seen dispersing high up in the clouds and everyone knew that the German pilots were choosing their targets. They began to dive. The men watched them with tense faces. They felt an immense, selfish relief, which they did not bother to hide, when they discovered that none of the bombers were diving on their ship.

For the first half of that day, none of the bombers chose *The City of Joliet*. The most violent attacks took place a long way off, and yet the men were exhausted. Their eyes were red and swollen ; they were deaf and shouted to make themselves heard even when the gunfire had ceased. As soon as the alert was over, the gunners lay down for a moment on the deck with their helmets over their eyes.

Other ships were hit by bombs and they smoked and blazed. The crew of *The City of Joliet* saw men clambering over the side, rowing away slowly, desperately slowly, in their poor vulnerable boats while the roaring and wailing of the dive bombers continued around them. Two of these floating braziers were left behind by the convoy and the escorting submarine put about to give them the *coup de grâce*. They were sunk from close quarters. The flaming hulls bucked and were engulfed, leaving a wisp of black smoke on the surface.

On board *The City of Joliet* the pumps were in action.

At midnight on the 26th May, the position of convoy PQ 16 was Lat. 73° 24′ N., Long. 9° 15′ E., in other words slightly NW of the North Cape and almost on the latitude of Bear Island. Its progress had been followed, not only by the crews of the merchant ships, but also by the Luftwaffe stationed at Bardufloss, Banar and Petsamo. The airmen had been given orders to attack the convoy without respite and as violently as possible, irrespective of the weather.

The meteorological conditions on the 27th May at 00.30 were as follows: " Dry, cold, calm sea, wind almost nil, stratus with a low ceiling." Eight torpedo-carrying aircraft were already in the air looking for the convoy. The last position given by the spotter aircraft dated from 22.30 of the 26th. The following day at 10.15, torpedo bombers picked up the convoy sailing on an easterly course close in to the ice pack.

As they approached, losing height, four of the destroyers broke off to meet them, firing all their guns. The pilots regained height, went above the clouds and came down again near the convoy. Each of them carried out his attack calmly and with determination, dropping his eggs from 3,000 feet. Two of the ships were hit by torpedoes and fell astern. The aircraft returned to base and reported their results.

Several bombers were ready to replace them. The Met announced an imminent improvement in the weather ; the Luftwaffe C.-in-C. based in Northern Norway, carrying out his orders, decided to hold back this squadron in order to carry out a decisive attack as soon as the sky cleared. The convoy advanced very slowly and the spotting aircraft kept it in sight. There was no risk involved in waiting to attack in the best possible conditions a target which, so to speak, was always within reach.

The improvement in the weather was slower than had been forecast, but the Met was optimistic and it was obvious that the cloud ceiling was breaking up. At 17.00 hours the reconnaissance aircraft gave the position of the convoy, adding that the two torpedoed ships had rejoined it.

The first wave of bombers was airborne between 07.45 and 08.15. Three-quarters of an hour later the convoy was sighted. The meteorological conditions were now: fine clear weather, sharp cold, brilliant sunshine, a slight south-easterly breeze, visibility unlimited.

The call to action stations had sounded at 09.00.

Today there are few people in Europe who cannot recall one of those mornings when they scanned the sky with anxiety, fearing to see the protective clouds vanish and a bright blue sky appear. Such is the folly of war. The crew of The City of Joliet had looked gratefully at the heavy ceiling of cloud: they had sworn and blasphemed when it began to break up. And now they abhorred the blue sky, the dazzling polar seascape with ships covered with glittering ice in the sun disgusted them. In this magnificent setting they felt wretched and naked.

The German planes were bright dots in the sky, very far to the South. After drawing close for a moment they changed course, flew parallel to the convoy, then broke away and disappeared over the horizon to the S.S.W., to reappear five minutes later on an easterly course. What was the meaning of the manoeuvre? At 09.30 several machines made for the convoy, gaining height. They were dive bombers.

Two main attacks took place on the 27th May between 09.40 and 22.00.

When one studies the log book entries and the survivors' accounts, it will be found that they were distinct attacks, but obviously for the sailors of PQ 16 the 27th May did not appear in its historical aspect as a succession of attacks with brief intervals. For them it was an almost uninterrupted nightmare which began at 09.40.

The terrible seconds while the bombers slowly dispersed above the convoy, each pilot choosing his target; the deadly seconds during which the men saw the wings of the diving aircraft growing larger. The interminable moments while they fought the fires that crept towards holds filled with explosives; the hours they worked in compartments below, stopping the leaks and shoring up twisted bulkheads —all these moments added up in their memory and their sensibilities, until the weight became more and more exhausting and unbearable. The dappled sky was dotted with black and white ack-ack bursts. The men, completely deafened, saw the fountains thrown up in the water by the bombs. The air reeked of gunpowder and the greyish-yellow smoke from the guns which the wind slowly dispersed. Through it they could see the red glow of fires. After the first attack two blazing vessels were abandoned. Astern of the convoy one of them had already been hit by a torpedo at 01.15.

The morning attacks took place at 10.25, 11.00 and 11.55 respectively. The attacking planes seemed inexhaustible and invulnerable. Eight dive bombers, six dive bombers, fifteen dive bombers . . . "They seemed to return in greater numbers each time," an officer in the corvette *Roselys* noted in his diary, "and yet we had brought down and seriously damaged some, which we hoped would not get home." Damaged, possibly, but apparently only one enemy aircraft was shot down in the course of these attacks —the one which crashed on the *Empire Lawrence,* as we shall describe later. The firing of the inexperienced gunners and machine-gunners in the merchant ships was inaccurate (later they, too, would shoot down aircraft; the fire power of the destroyers was insufficient to cover the whole convoy. Moreover, the German airmen who attacked these Arctic convoys were first-class pilots.

In the course of the attack at 11.00 one of the bombers dropped a stick of bombs on *The City of Joliet* from less than a thousand feet (the Junkers could carry sixteen fifty-pounders). The crew saw them falling obliquely and rather slowly. The pilot did not pull out as soon as he had dropped his load: he merely decreased his dive and continued towards the deck, machine-gunning as he came down. Green flames spurted from his wings. On the deck, one of the temporary wooden gangways built over the piled-up vehicles to allow the crew to circulate, caught fire. The bombs fell in the sea all round the ship. The Junkers streaked like a meteor over the deck at a hundred feet. They felt that they could almost have touched the huge black crosses bordered with white. They could see every detail of the aircraft, even the pilot sitting in his cockpit. The crew saw his broad shoulders, head and goggles. It was strange to see an enemy airman at such close quarters. The Junkers did a thunderous zoom, still firing with its rear guns. Round, light-edged holes appeared on the new paint of the petrol trucks. The men put out the fire on the wooden gangway which was blazing peacefully. An hour later another bomber dived on their ship. The pilot released his bomb, this time a large one, from less than five hundred feet. The Liberty ship, whose helm was hard over to port at the beginning of the dive, was now swinging to starboard. The work of the helmsman was exhausting during these attacks because of the waterproof suit which hampered his movements and made him sweat. Beneath this garment, too, the men wore the life-jacket. It would have been ideal to wear several light garments one over the other to avoid perspiring, but this waterproof suit was a safeguard. The bomb fell in the sea thirty yards to port, making the ship shudder. At 11.25 the chief engineer told the captain that the water was pouring in and gaining on the pumps. The attacks continued.

In the galley one of the negro mess boys made some coffee. During the first attacks all the cooks and coloured boys had cowered in corners. The crew had only been able to eat cold rations with never a hot dish or a hot drink. But now a few of the cooks went on with their work even during the attacks. When a near miss made the ship shiver they stopped and went over to the door, only to return to their galley when it was all clear. Others sat down against the bulkheads, occasionally getting up to give their mates a hand.

In a nearby gangway some of the white men, in their waterproof suits, fastened at the neck, were lying against the pipes. Their faces were white and drawn. The negroes looked ashen in colour. When one of the mess boys passed carrying a tray or a jug, their eyes followed him but they did not move from their position.

A few men sat in the mess, eating and drinking coffee. Shorty related that when he was off duty he often went to the mess during attacks to get a bite to eat and a cup of coffee. He usually carried his life-jacket and waterproof suit. The men sat round the table in silence. They too stood up and made for the door when a more than usually violent explosion shook the ship. Some of them went out and returned later. It is easy to realize that Shorty once more regretted having hoisted his kitbag aboard one of these cargo vessels destined for the Arctic Ocean at the end of his last leave.

Sometimes the attack finished before Shorty had to return below the engine room. Usually he lay down in his bunk with all his clothes on and his life-saving kit within reach of his hand. But sometimes he had to return to his watch while an attack was still in progress. He admitted that more than once he had hoped that a bomb would hit *The City of Joliet* without blowing up the ship or killing him. Then the order to abandon ship would be given and the crew would be picked up by an escort vessel, as many others had been. Then he would not have to go down to the engine room again.

The attacks now were almost uninterrupted. At 12.45 hours one of their neighbours, the *Michigan,* just avoided a salvo of bombs. Several of the vessels were zig-zagging in all directions. Two minutes later a couple of Junkers dived in succession on another vessel, the *Empire Lawrence.* The crew of *The City of Joliet* saw the ship bearing down on them like a hunted beast. The bombs from the first plane all fell in the sea. The second had no time to drop his. Hit by the ack-ack, he continued to plummet like a stone until he crashed with a terrible explosion on the bows of the cargo ship.

An enormous column of seething black smoke billowed in the air. When it dispersed they saw that the *Empire Lawrence* was listing badly by the bows. Her stem post was only a few feet above the water. On deck a group of brand new trucks were on fire and the crew were running from this curtain of flame. The boats were lowered over the side and the rafts were thrown overboard. (These rafts lay flat on the deck without being secured. They were often stacked on an incline so that they could slide on their own into the sea.) The crew jumped into the water without waiting any longer. Unfortunately, in the rush several rafts had not been held alongside and floated away from the drifting ship. The men who had jumped into the sea had to swim a long time to reach them.

The *Empire Lawrence* passed quite close to *The City of Joliet* and they could see the unfortunate men swimming in the icy water. The boats drew slowly away from the wreck. The exhausted swimmers seemed to find it terribly hard to hoist themselves up on the rafts. When they were exhausted they stretched out their arms piteously to their mates. They could see their white faces and even the fear in their eyes. Their cries could not be heard above the noise of the gunfire but they were obviously screaming.

There was no question of stopping and picking them up. No merchant ship was allowed to do this and the orders were categorical. They had to sail on averting their eyes from these wretched men struggling in the water. Moreover, above the convoy other bombers had just broken formation and were selecting their targets.

A corvette at last arrived steaming at full speed for the *Empire Lawrence*. The cargo boat suddenly sank lower in the water and disappeared in a mighty eddy. The corvette began to circle the spot to pick up the survivors. Two Junkers dived on it, dropping their bombs and machine-gunning the vessel. Fortunately all the bombs missed, but corpses could now be seen floating in the water in bright yellow waterproof suits.

At 14.15 the British destroyer *H.M.S. Ashanti*, the escort leader, sent a signal to the corvette *Roselys* of the Free French Naval Forces[1]: " Go and help the *Starye Bolchevik*."

The Soviet vessel was lagging behind the convoy under a huge umbrella of black smoke. On close inspection the

[1] Formerly the *Sundew*, 925 tons. The corvettes were small solid escort vessels of the whaler type mass produced in the British naval dockyards. They were armed with a 102 mm gun, several oerlikons and machine-guns and two grenade throwers (twelve grenades).

flames could be seen. When the corvette drew to within twenty yards of her the Captain used his megaphone and explained in English that a bomb had hit the *Starye Bolchevik* and caused a number of casualties, dead and wounded. The bomb had also destroyed the fire fighting apparatus. The Russian vessel was loaded with T.N.T. and other explosives.

The *Roselys* drew in to ten yards and managed to convey hoses to the " old Bolshevik." While the two vessels sailed side by side a new air attack developed. Luckily no aircraft dived in their direction. Within a short while the fire was under control.

At 15.20 there was another attack by eight dive bombers. The Commodore's ship was hit. Although flames. rose from the bows the ship did not sink and kept its position. A moment later, however, he sent a signal: "The Commodore is transferring his flag to the *Alynbank.*"

In most of the ships' logs one finds this entry more or less in the same language: "Another vessel of the convoy in the starboard column was hit."

This ship was *The City of Joliet.*

Shorty saw the bomb coming.

He was not on watch but having a snack in the mess. All the men there heard the drone of the dive bomber which as it increased developed into a wail. Less than a second later they were all on their feet rushing for the door. Shorty cannot remember how he got on deck. He only remembers that he was outside when he noticed the aircraft and the bomb. The scream of the Junkers' siren, the gunfire and machine-gun fire made such an infernal din that it made him tremble. The plane showed its belly and the bomb appeared like a khaki balloon against the blue sky.

He lay flat on the deck and bumped against one of his shipmates. The explosion of the bomb and the bucking of the ship raised him off the deck. He found himself three yards away with his right side bruised against the track of a tank. Ahead of him yellow flames had sprung up surrounded with dense black smoke. Shorty could not say whether the fire was ten or forty yards away from him. A few moments later he noticed that the bows were on fire. Then he realized that he was on his feet leaning against the tank putting on his life-saving costume. He had put on the woollen waistcoat without noticing it. In all the buffeting he had not lost a single of his treasures.

The engines stopped. The gun in the stern was still firing. Men were running about the deck, some forward some aft and others towards the boats. Shorty followed the latter. He saw that they had already begun to lower Nos. 2 and 3 boats. Near a davit stood another greaser, a pal of Shorty's, in his overalls. He was bent double with a fit of coughing, but kept clutching his life-saving gear. His eyes were red and watering. A sailor told Shorty that the greaser had just come up from the engine room. The shock of the explosion had released some ammonia from a tank, spreading the suffocating fumes.

There were no flames to be seen now in the bows, only smoke. The men began to get into the boats. At that moment the Second Mate arrived and said: " You can start to embark but don't panic. The order to abandon ship hasn't yet been given." Nevertheless he handed his sextant in its box to one of the sailors. The boats were lowered.

Several men had literally flung themselves into the boats and now sat huddled on the thwarts with glassy eyes, paralysed by fear. Others who appeared quite calm prevented them from shipping water. The two boats rose and fell on the swell alongside the hull. At the masthead of *The City of Joliet* a signal was flown: " Vessel out of control."

The period of waiting in the boats bobbing up and down by the hull seemed interminable. The guns of the convoy ships continued to fire but those of *The City of*

Joliet had almost ceased. She had now fallen astern, and the attack was moving away from her. This situation was both reassuring and alarming. The attack had gone further away but these aircraft would certainly spot this motionless lone vessel. They could return in a few seconds. The men in the whalers began to suffer from the cold and their teeth started to chatter. An officer looked over the side.

"You're to return aboard. All men to their action stations."

The Captain and the Chief Engineer of *The City of Joliet* had been down into the engine room in gas masks and had explored the bottom. They both came to the conclusion that the damage was not irreparable. The leak in the ammonia tank was being repaired and the ventilator fans were sucking up the unhealthy vapours. The bomb which had fallen in the bows had not smashed a bulkhead. All the damage seemed repairable. Everyone back to his post, then.

When they heard this some of the men began to swear, others to cry and groan. The idea of returning to their ship was unbearable now that they had been on the point of leaving her. Naturally they would have been no safer in another ship, but they were all more or less convinced that by leaving their own they were fleeing from danger. Nevertheless the order was carried out despite the oaths and groans. The boats were hauled inboard.

The very moment the first man stepped on deck the guns began to fire at two Junkers which streaked across the sky with a thunderous roar a few feet above the masthead. The men fell flat with beating hearts. But these aircraft dropped no bombs and did not use their machineguns.

Several of those who had re-embarked were sick with weariness and emotion. The chief cook lay inert in one of the boats. He had to be carried aboard. At last *The City of Joliet* was able to get under way. She had a slight list to starboard and was down by the bows but she sailed at normal speed.

At 17.35 the corvette *Roselys* arrived alongside and asked if she wanted any help. The Captain replied that he had shored up the bulkheads of the threatened watertight compartments.

" I hope we shall make it," he said.

Five minutes later eight aircraft arrived in regular formation from the south. Their arrival heralded the start of a combined attack by torpedo-carrying planes, dive bombers and U-boats.

Time lost its meaning, there was no continuity in events and, so to speak, no more convoy. A scattered mêlée of ships zig-zagging wildly about the sea like drunken men . . . A sky filled with ack-ack bursts ; destroyers weaving at full speed blowing their whistles, among the geysers ; the white blossoms of bursting bombs, white fountains from bursting depth charges and the slim scars of torpedoes coming from all directions—that is what the PQ 16 had become. There were several U-boats inside the convoy.

The gunners saw a periscope, a second and a third. A ship's engines suddenly stopped, she began to list and would shortly sink ; two others were on fire. The torpedo aircraft attacked the convoy from starboard and astern. The dive bombers screamed down from all directions.

When one reads the log books and the accounts of the two attacks which took place between 17.40 and 18.50— they both tally and leave no doubt as to the intensity of the action—one cannot conceive why the PQ 16 did not lose an important part of her effectives. It is a known fact that until 18.40 not a single ship sank. On the 27th May at 18.35 the convoy had so far lost only four ships since setting sail (not counting the ship that had returned to Iceland ; the two stragglers left in flames after the 09.40 attack had just rejoined the convoy). Apparently several vessels which were hit were momentarily abandoned, re-manned and got under way after the fires had been put out.

On board *The City of Joliet* (as on all the others) the men were exhausted from weariness and nervous tension ; they were either prostrate (a few of them), had become automata or galvanised by whisky. Most of them had had no real sleep for weeks.

At 18.40 a vessel loaded with explosives was hit by a stick of bombs. The dread column of fire spurted skywards.

It spread out into a gigantic egg of flame and the changes of colour were its tragic apotheosis. It was like a huge bouquet of all these tracers fired into the air, the epitome of all conflagrations. When the glare died away and the faint smoke vanished no trace remained where the vessel had once been. The aircraft flew off and the guns ceased firing. Some shrapnel still fell, ricocheting off the plates or plunging like knives into the water. The gunners fell back almost unconscious beside their guns. The sky started to become overcast.

A new attack took place at 20.30 almost entirely concentrated on the destroyer *H.M.S. Garland* which was sailing at the head of the convoy. She was hit by bombs and machine-gunned. At 20.50 she sent a signal to *H.M.S. Ashanti*: "Seventeen killed, twenty-nine wounded. Ackack out of action." The *Ashanti* replied: " You can go." The *Garland* put on speed and made her way alone to Murmansk.

By 22.00 the convoy had almost reformed. A layer of protective clouds now covered it. The crews could not believe in such a stroke of luck.

The City of Juliet was worth a million and a half dollars ; the cargo more than twenty millions. For as long as possible the Captain had dismissed the idea of letting all this wealth go to the bottom of the sea. But in the early morning of the 28th he was forced to think about it. The ship had to be abandoned.

The hull was divided into seven watertight compartments. Beneath the pressure of the water which had entered by the breach in the bows two of them had collapsed and another was buckled. In spite of the pumps the water also seeped through the chinks in the damaged plates into the bottom, the engine and boiler rooms. If another bulkhead suddenly gave way the ship might sink at once as a result of the boilers bursting.

Preparations to abandon ship were made during this lull. Now that the attackers had gone, most of the men— including Shorty—said that they were sorry to leave their ship. They knew that they could only take with them their papers and perhaps a little linen. They would have to leave most of their possessions, the modest objects so dear to all sailors. Twelve hours before they had only thought of saving their skins, but now they were regretting the loss of a few material objects.

Since she was now shipping more water, the order to abandon ship was given.

The City of Joliet sank in the Arctic Ocean with its full load of aircraft, tanks, vehicles and ammunition. The crew was picked up by the *Roselys.*

Two rather feeble attacks were launched on the 28th May at 09.45 and 11.00. The low ceiling and fog protected the convoy. The Russian destroyers met it during the morning.

At 11.00, still hugging the ice pack, the convoy at Long.3°22′E., a little west of the Murmansk meridian, reached the highest latitude of its trip: 74°15′N. To find this on the map it is necessary to look at the sheet marked Arctic Circle. This particular part of the ocean is known as the Barents Sea.

On several occasions the drone of aircraft flying above the clouds was heard. The men thanked Heaven for this protective covering and sailed on with relief into the heart of the icy fog.

A great silence had replaced the din of firing and

explosions. The decks, rigging and superstructures were now covered with ice, transforming them into phantom ships. These ghosts glided slowly across a sea of dreams carrying brand new warlike toys, covered with the same icy veneer glistening in the diffused light.

Below decks, however, stark reality reigned. The mess decks and cabins were damp and streaming with water. The clothes of those who came below immediately began to thaw and dry as soon as the ice melted from them. Although the messes were well heated this damp could never be prevented. Every effort had been made to stop this perpetual sweating of the bulkheads by covering them with a preparation of asbestos. The men fought against the cold and damp by constantly drinking hot toddies.

Although the icy fog brought some respite to the men, navigation was by no means made easier. The captains hardly dared to leave the bridge any more than they had during the attacks. Icebergs often appeared on this pallid sea which was dotted with numerous flows and ice blocks. It may perhaps be of interest to describe here the nature of the ice to be met with in Arctic seas.

Floating ice can originate from three sources: mountain glaciers, rivers and sea water. Freshwater ice (from glaciers and rivers) can be distinguished from salt water ice by its hardness which is at the same time brittle, by its greater transparency and by its colour which is slightly bluish or greenish.

The glaciers of the polar regions reach down to the sea. From their fringe are born the icebergs, blue or green in colour, shrouded in mist and a belt of intense cold. It is known that their draught is equal to between four and six times the ice exposed. It is prudent to give them a wide berth as their submerged area is sometimes very large. The great maritime disasters caused by icebergs are well known.

The formation of seawater ice is more complicated and of greater interest.

As a result of a fall in temperature or after a snowfall that cools the sea (freezing point of salt water is $-1.6°$ to $-2.5°$) one sees crystals forming on the calm or slightly rippled surface. In very calm weather a mist rises—sailors call it " a smoking sea." These crystals congeal into curds which form a frozen brew of ice and snow mixed (slush ice or grease). The sea is then covered with a steel grey or leaden grey layer like melted grease growing cold. If the cold increases, this icy brew congeals and the calm patches are covered by a fine layer of ice. The congelation is not always uniform ; it produces strange discs fifteen to twenty-five inches in diameter with raised edges. This is the reason why this formation is known as pancake ice. If the wind blows and whips up the sea the icy brew congeals in white pieces: this is iced mud or crumbly ice.

Should the cold spell persist, each expanse of ice thickens and congeals ; the icepack thus begins to form. Any vast conglomeration of seawater ice is called an ice-pack. The violent wind, the swell and the waves break the ice-pack into a variety of expanses—the icefields which extend as far as the eye can see ; floes which cover an area of a square mile ; ice blocks of one to a hundred yards square. Any marine ice which has drifted from its original position is called the ice-pack.

The floating ice-packs driven by a stiff breeze collide ; their edges rise and straddle each other, form the tortured chaos or hammocks. The fragments detached from these formations are known as floebergs. They are sometimes confused with icebergs which, as I have already mentioned, have been formed from fresh water.

Polar explorers often meet rounded iceblocks of medium size which have broken off from floebergs and icebergs. They call these " growlers " or " tubs." These medium blocks are dangerous because they have very little ice showing above the water.

The jagged blocks of marine ice are called " swans." The iceblocks are baby icebergs.

Convoy PQ 16 sailed south through all this ice on the 28th and 29th May—*i.e.* during those forty-eight hours of continual daylight. The ships had to manoeuvre the entire time. The escort vessels did their best to see that the slow procession was not broken up, this convoy of which they could only see a part on the whitish water.

On the morning of the 28th the fog grew denser until visibility was reduced to a hundred yards. The ships lost sight of each other and began to sail whenever this was possible by the fog buoy towed by the vessel ahead. More often than not they saw absolutely nothing. They had to sail a general course and manoeuvre to avoid the ice, listening for their neighbours' sirens which were muffled by the fog.

At the end of the day the fog lightened and dispersed. None of the ships had got lost. The captains already seemed to have grown used to this type of navigation. Some but not all of them had had previous experience. They were all old salts. The Higher Authorities still hesitated to entrust the command of ships sailing in the Arctic Ocean to young officers chosen for their physical reflexes and capacity for taking a decision, who often proved to be so outstanding. The old sea dogs, in spite of their obstinacy and their many failings, were without exception better equipped to adapt themselves to this kind of navigation than anyone else.

About 20.00 on the 29th " Snoopy Joe " came out of the clouds. The cam-ship catapulted its fighter to go and attack it. The hawk was immediately shot down. Twelve Dorniers suddenly appeared at this moment. The fighter pilot flew at once to meet them. The guns which had started to fire had to cease fire. On the decks of the merchant vessels men began to shout, treating the British pilot as a lunatic (I have been unable to discover his name), then fell silent, hardly daring to watch the unequal combat he was waging. A minute later he was shot down.

He baled out but when the ship picked him up he was dead, riddled with bullets.

From 22.00 onwards seven dive bombers attacked the convoy at intervals of twenty minutes. Several ships, having no ammunition left, could not fire. None was hit.

On 30th May, about 03.00, a few ships destined for Archangel, east of Murmansk in the White Sea, left the convoy. From 06.00 to 08.00 isolated dive bombers attacked the convoy without result. Now the men were eager to reach port; they had had enough; they could not have borne the idea of a renewed attack. At 08.10 a formation appeared; thirty aircraft. The crews groaned and swore. Some in ships which had no ammunition left wanted to jump over the side. Notwithstanding, a few ships started to fire. The escort leader sent a swift signal with his Aldis lamp: "Cease fire. They're Russians." The gunners recognised Hurricanes and other small planes with red stars on their wings.

At last there were signs that they were approaching land: floating tree trunks and land birds. At 11.00 they sighted the coast. A little later it grew more easily defined: it was dark, rocky and covered with pines.

High hills flank the Gulf of Kola into which the Murmansk river flows. South of Letinski promontory they could see bare cliffs. To the west of the entrance the shore consisted of red cliffs which further south gave place to mossy hills covered with shrubs.

At 13.00 the merchant ships formed into line ahead to enter the river Murmansk. Russian pilots came aboard. They were nearly all young officers of the Russian Navy in dark grey uniforms with unsmiling faces. Those who spoke a few words of English explained that they were detailed for this job of pilotage when they were not on watch or when their ships happened to be in port.

Most of the crews had never seen Murmansk before. They stared with curiosity at these desolate shores where no harbour was visible. At last the concrete buildings on the outskirts of the town and the first quays along the river's edge came into view.

Teams of workmen were busy unloading trucks. They saw the workers busy at their work, some in civilian clothes and others in uniform ; some had bandaged heads. There were women among them in trousers or peasant skirts. They humped the cases just as well as the men.

CHAPTER FOUR

The Russian Ports

ANY NEW TOWN SEEN FROM THE DECK OF A ship arouses the excitement of the unknown. The traveller scans the shore and imagines it may be a dream port of call. But when he goes ashore he often finds nothing but a wretched village.

The sailors of convoy PQ 16 could see that Murmansk was no village. Beyond the jetties concrete buildings rose to three, four and five storeys ; not in alignment but dotted all over the place at irregular intervals. They seemed dead ; no one at the windows, no washing hanging out, not a sign of life. Not a soul round the houses or on the quayside. Other buildings stood higher up on the hills, also spread out with great empty spaces between them. They could see the ruins of houses destroyed by bombing. Murmansk appeared dead beneath a low leaden sky. It was raining.

To be precise the town seemed unreal. This is the word which is frequently to be found in the accounts of eye witnesses and it was first uttered to me by a British Naval officer whom I questioned at length about Murmansk.

" We felt we were in another world," he said, " in an unreal world."

The ships were sent first to moor some way up the Murmansk river, officially to allow the crews a period of rest ; in reality to wait for cranes to become available. The port installations were inadequate for this traffic.

Twenty-four hours after arrival a cargo vessel descended as far as the harbour. She came alongside to unload her ammunition.

The Murmansk quays were as surprising as the town itself. A terrible disorder reigned and filth lay everywhere —refuse, old iron, broken crates and parts of demolished trucks, potato peelings and excrement.

The cranes began to unload the ammunition. Russian workers carried the cases to the railway trucks not far away. The gangs included soldiers, civilians and women. The sailors soon learned that the soldiers were men on leave, slightly wounded or convalescing, and that the civilians were political prisoners. There were almost as many women as men and they worked just as hard ; the younger ones were strapping wenches with legs like telegraph poles.

The crews were surprised to see that the jetty was deserted except for the strip where they were unloading. Normally the quays of a port are a hive of activity. Here there was none. Only this gang of workers and on either side of them the filthy quayside, silent and deserted.

They also found the behaviour of the dockers extremely odd. Both the military and the civilians would be working normally and then suddenly something appeared to go wrong. Impossible to discover what. The cranes stopped and the man on the crane began to slang the team on the jetty. Men and women joined in and everyone gesticulated wildly with great volubility. This lasted for an interminable time and no one could find out the trouble. Then for no apparent reason work was resumed.

Or again at unpredictable intervals everyone stopped working. The workers sat down on the crates or on heaps of rubble and ate slices of black bread or other strange food, indefinable at a distance. During this break both men and women, without bothering to move off, relieved nature without the slightest embarrassment. . . .

The rain had stopped. The seamen looked anxiously up at the sky from time to time, fearing to see their protective covering disappear. They could not understand why the Russians refused to use the ships' derricks and winches to speed up this laborious unloading. They would willingly have given a hand to these workers even without being paid. But this was strictly forbidden. The Soviet authorities in Murmansk always opposed the use of ship's equipment and the help of the crew for unloading.

Finally the last crate was ashore. The vessel left the ammunition quay for the opposite bank where the war material was to be unloaded.

She manoeuvred slowly under the orders of a Russian pilot. The ship had just passed the middle of the stream when a dull explosion shook her, raising the water around her. The engines stopped. She listed heavily to starboard with steam coming from her hull. She had just hit a magnetic mine.

Three good minutes elapsed. The ship's company ran up on deck but the harbour remained deserted ; nothing stirred ashore. On the war material jetty a few Russians stood watching the scene quite impassively. The vessel was apparently going to be left to sink in the middle of this grey river amidst general indifference.

At last a launch appeared at full speed. It rounded the cargo boat and stopped. The men aboard in fur coats and military caps, yelled in Russian to the pilot who was leaning over the rail. He yelled back at them and a shouting match started. The conversation was interminable and the crew wondered what they had to talk about when the situation was so obvious. The cargo vessel was now listing by the stern. The Captain seized his megaphone and addressed the Russians in English.

Eventually a tug left the shore, took up its position at the bows and the hawser secured. The water foamed behind the tug but the cargo boat would not move. She was too heavy as a result of the water she had shipped. The Captain shouted to the Russians that a second tug should be sent immediately. The launch sped away towards the shore.

A boat was lowered to put ashore several wounded and two dead who had just been brought up from the engine room. The crew were livid with despair. It was futile to have brought all this material at the risk of their lives to see it sink ignominiously in the Murmansk river.

Just as the lifeboat touched the water, the sirens wailed and the ack-ack went into action. The destroyers anchored a little downstream joined in with the shore batteries. Five aircraft came out of the clouds and dived on the railway station and the jetties on the left bank. There were loud explosions. After about two minutes the guns ceased firing ; the Russian fighters were airborne, but the enemy planes were already far away. A fire was raging near the station.

The second tug had arrived. The launch which had returned left again immediately towing the boat with the wounded and the two dead. Meanwhile the merchant vessel continued to sink.

The two tugs were making every effort but it was obvious that they were too late. The ship's company began to get into the other two lifeboats. The tugs continued for a few moments. The Captain and three officers were still in the bows of the cargo vessel leaning over the side. It was useless. She remained motionless on the grey water which soon reached the level of the after deck.

The Captain himself with the help of his officers threw overboard large hawsers which fell with a bang and a splash. The vessel sank with its entire load of trucks and tanks. From the quay the Russians watched her sink without uttering a word or making a movement.

A party of seamen from Convoy PQ 16 was invited to dinner by the People's Foreign Trade Commissar, Kovalsky. He was a rather short dark man with a pleasant face beneath his grey astrakhan cap. He wore a long overcoat with an astrakhan collar and boots.

The weather was cold, foggy and rainy. Kovalsky took his visitors first to see the official monuments. They were shown " The House of Rest and Culture," a large white concrete building. In front of it had been left a bare space which in any other part of the world except the Arctic Circle would have been a park. A huge statue of Lenin stood in the place of honour, and in front of it a twin-engined Messerschmitt which had been shot down. The seamen examined the statue and the trophy.

" Now let's go and eat," Kovalsky said brightly. " You will see the Arctic Hotel."

In June, 1942, the gangs of roadsweepers could not clear the Murmansk streets of rubble and old iron. Half the ruined town was still inhabited. All the seamen, particularly the Americans, were struck by the sight of these labour gangs working in the rain. They were composed of men, women and children. " In front of the Arctic Hotel were a score of women the youngest of whom must have been fifty. They were busy digging holes and planting telegraph poles in them." Other teams loaded rubble, stones and refuse into trucks while others built shelters.

In the hall of the Arctic Hotel stood four enormous stone brown bears, one in each corner. A few Russian officers and some Allied soldiers and sailors of all ranks were sitting in the armchairs smoking and drinking.

" You see how pleasant the place is," said Kovalsky. " We have a barber's shop, too, over there. You can come here as often as you like and you will always be welcome."

The People's Commissar obviously could not foresee that precisely one week later the Arctic Hotel would be reduced to rubble in an air raid.

He led his guests to the dining room where a meal was served of caviare, fish, meat and rice, with plenty of vodka and white wine. Kovalsky entertained his guests with stories of Russia's immense war effort, quoting figures and mentioning what they had just seen for themselves—all the citizens working without respite in the harshest possible conditions. That aspect needed no explanation. For the men who had arrived from the United States or even from Great Britain, this barracks in the Arctic Circle was still a novel surprise and they much admired the courage and tenacity of the inhabitants. Then other subjects were broached. At the end of the meal guests tried to joke with the waitresses.

76

"Ah," said Kovalsky, "you must be serious here. Our Soviet code of morals is very strict. Any Soviet woman who gives herself to a foreigner is severely punished. But you will find other distractions. Each Saturday evening, for example, there is a 500-voice male choir at the House of Rest and Culture. The concert takes place even if the bombs are falling. The choir leader comes each week from Leningrad whether there is a raid or not. I'm certain you'll enjoy them."

The sailors showed a very lukewarm enthusiasm. Kovalsky added that they could also visit the International Club where they would meet " girls with whom they could talk and dance."

This proposal met with great applause and most of them went the same day to this club.

One reads in certain journalists' articles of this period that the girls were very pretty and smart, that they danced beautifully and spoke fluent English; the sailors had a fine time at the International Club dancing and in polite conversation with their partners. All later witnesses I have managed to approach directly gave me quite another version of this fraternisation. The girls of the International Club understood very little English; they were under surveillance and so strictly guarded that they hardly dared to smile. They danced like sticks of wood in their partners' arms. The men were so disappointed that after an hour they were all dancing together—and obviously that had not been the original idea of the party. None of them paid a second visit to this Club. One wonders why the Soviet authorities had taken the trouble to open it and to send the girls there. The Allied seamen understood it no more than they understood the general behaviour of the Russians.

At the outset there were a few receptions exchanged between Russian and Allied officers in the warships. A British destroyer officer described one of these to me. With his brother officers he was invited aboard a Soviet destroyer.

The Russians offered them several rounds of vodka and in a mixture of Russian and English began to propose toasts to Marshal Stalin, etc. . . . The Russians drank heavily and their guests had to empty their glasses in one gulp. At the end of the festivities one of the British officers proposed a toast to His Majesty King George VI, since none of the Russians had thought of doing so. The Soviet officers drank the toast, with the exception of one who flung his glass on the floor, spat on it and broke into a torrent of incomprehensible abuse. Since by this time everyone was slightly intoxicated, the British officers had the good taste to ignore the incident and to attribute it to the vodka. The party broke up a little later and the British returned to their ship, which was tied up against the quay.

The following day a large armed party arrived on the jetty. The Captain of the destroyer, prepared for any eventuality, gave the order: "Action stations." (" This will give you some idea of the atmosphere reigning in Murmansk," said my informant. " We were always prepared to hear that the U.S.S.R. had turned against the Allies, and we felt that we might be arrested or attacked at any moment.")

When the party reached the destroyer, the Soviet troops halted, and the ranks opened to disclose a man dressed in a pair of trousers and a shirt. Facing the ship, this man pronounced a kind of speech in Russian. Then he was marched over to a shed and shot before the eyes of the stupefied British sailors. It was later learned that the victim was the naval officer who had made a scene when the toast to the King of England had been proposed. He had just been shot as a disciplinary measure.

The Russians were definitely trigger-happy. On several occasions, officers and Allied seamen only escaped the bullets of the patrols by the skin of their teeth ; these soldiers were apt to fire at anything they saw. The sentries often refused categorically to examine the passes which were handed to them or, being illiterates, held them upside down.

The Allied ships at Murmansk were not allowed to use their radio. All their communications had to pass through the Soviet authorities. The sailors were never allowed to leave the environs of Murmansk—even those who were stranded there for several months. Admiral W. H. Standley, United States Ambassador in Russia, after long parleys, managed to arrange for a few ships' captains and high-ranking officers to visit Moscow as his personal guests.

On several occasions the British High Command suggested to the Soviet that one or several R.A.F. squadrons should be based at Murmansk to reinforce their defences and to bomb the German airfields in Northern Norway. The Russians invariably refused the offer.

The nearest German airfield was forty miles away, in other words, a bare ten minutes' flight. As soon as the weather cleared, the sirens wailed and the German bombers came into view over the hills. The Russian fighters rarely had time to get into the air before the bombs fell.

Nevertheless, the unloading of the ships proceeded in the same muddle and at the same slow tempo. Apart from the basic inefficiency (" The Russians are capable of carrying out gigantic tasks and have done so," said my informant, " but at the cost of a wastage and human effort which is terrifying to Westerners.") the dockers at Murmansk seemed bound by incomprehensible restrictions. The Allied sailors were often furious at having to wait an interminable time before orders to start unloading were given, although the quayside was free, the crane in position, and the male and female workers waiting on the quay. Once, the crew of a ship, infuriated at having to wait not a matter of hours or a few days but a whole month, dumped all the material on a big ice block with their own derricks. When the last army truck had been unloaded, the port officials arrived, shouting, sending tugs and gesticulating . . .

One sees today that the Soviet authorities at Murmansk

were never able to indoctrinate the Allied crews. Kovalsky's invitation was merely a gesture of official courtesy, quite incomprehensible taking into account the behaviour of the Russians in general. It is certain that for the Communist or " fellow traveller " sailors (and there were quite a few) their stay in Murmansk was a deception followed by complete ideological immunisation. The thought of Russia's great achievements and war effort was not enough to make them forget what they could see with their own eyes—the appalling conditions in which her nationals lived.

This poverty was in fact at the root of the personal relationships that formed between the British and American sailors and the Russian ordinary men and women despite bans and difficulties. The Russians offered vodka in exchange for food and clothes. The inhabitants received the sailors to their homes after taking the greatest precautions. This barter brought about relations of another kind but rarely. Sailors caught *in flagrante delictu* or simply in a mild flirtation were escorted back to their ships at the point of a tommy-gun. Some were detained for a few days in the local police stations, and this cooled their ardour.

It would have been surprising had the black market not led to quite a number of troubles. Sailors were punished for several days' absence without leave, drunkenness or refusing to work on board, for thefts of food and rations from the lifeboats. Captain S. B. Franckel, Naval Attaché in Northern Russia, had to jail several sailors for more serious offences.

We must not lose sight of the fact that a certain number of these men had signed on for these Arctic voyages because of the extremely high pay and bonuses. They eventually found it hard to fulfil the conditions of their contract. It was probably among these men that we must look for the saboteurs of whom the documents make discreet mention. On the other hand, in these same documents we find many examples of efficiency, great courage and ingenuity shown by both officers and crews. Had they not shown these qualities, the unloading would have been even more lengthy and the losses more considerable.

The Arctic Hotel was destroyed on the 10th June; not a wall was left standing. The undamaged head of one of the brown bears seemed to roar in silence, baring his fangs while the corpses were being dug out. Among the dead were several sailors from PQ 16.

The distractions of Murmansk proving more and more disappointing, the Captains of several ships and particularly the officers of the escort vessels tried to distract the crew by organising sporting events: rowing contests in whalers, sailing regattas, canoeing in Carley floats. Every prisoner-of-war (the sailors of PQ 16 really looked upon themselves as prisoners) knows the virtue of such distractions: an hour or two's forgetfulness and the full weight of boredom returns. But they were two hours won, said the organisers, and perhaps they were right. An air raid warning often interrupted these regattas at Murmansk.

The most surprising episode was furnished by the sailors of the corvette *Roselys,* which took part in one of these " slaloms " on rafts. Among her ship's company were a few natives from Tahiti and Noumea. As soon as the starting revolver was fired, rowing in perfect rhythm, they began to sing a Polynesian chant. The icy grey water echoed their deep harmonious voices. The seamen,. huddled against the dripping rails, and the Russians, motionless on the fire-blackened quays, listened in silence as if they were watching some magic ritual being performed to the song of the South Seas in the dark Arctic Circle.

A small part of the convoy PQ 16 had been sent on to Archangel. This port, on the right bank of the Dvina, is twenty-five miles from its mouth. The Dvina flows into the White Sea through a forty miles' wide delta which branches into numerous streams, with about 150 islands. Its marshy swamps are covered with stunted willows which are flooded by the spring tides. Hosts of seabirds fly over these waters.

The ships at first dropped anchor off Iokanka, the little port at the entrance to the White Sea, where they took on Russian pilots. These men looked like Mongols, spoke very little English and seemed to lack experience. They came aboard in pairs, one of them piloting and the other remaining silent.

When the vessels began to make their way up the Dvina, the sailors thought that they were entering some desolate region of China rather than Russia. On the banks, covered with scrub, nothing was to be seen except a few wooden huts round which huddled very old peasants. They looked exhausted and were clothed in colourless rags.

One of the ships went aground. The Mongolian pilot spent two hours trying to get her off but with no result. At last, to the amazement of the crew, he began to weep. His comrade had remained quite impassive and silent without interfering. One of the sailors, who had already visited Archangel, explained to the Captain that Mongol No. 2 was not a pilot: he was only there to observe his comrade's behaviour. This was the custom. The spy reported to the authorities the behaviour of the pilot with foreigners, and this was why the unfortunate Mongol No. 1 had burst into tears. The Captain of the vessel then resumed command of his own ship and got her off the sandbank.

Most of the ships received orders to anchor at Brevennik, a kind of outer port to Archangel. There were only wooden landing stages. Not a shop, not a café, no house worthy of the name: only a few huts. And the only people to be seen were the same exhausted-looking wretchedly dressed old men, who hardly glanced at the ships.

Half an hour after their arrival, however, there was an enormous crowd on these wooden quays. It was an amazing crowd composed exclusively of children, nearly all boys, dressed in incredible costumes—sheepskins, blankets with a hole for the head to go through, torn military tunics and even rags which might have been the remnants of liveries from the old regime. None of them wore shoes. This crowd milled about on the quayside below the ships, giving little swallow-like cries, jumping and stretching out their arms. "Tovarich Schokolad! Tovarich Papyrussa!" they cried. Oddly enough these children were not begging, as the sailors at first thought. No, they were holding out bundles of roubles. And they had more in their pockets, and they showed these pockets swollen with notes as they continued to yell: "Tovarich Schokolad! Tovarich Papyrussa!" So there was a black market even at Brevennik, and these children were the speculators!

The official rate of exchange was twenty roubles to the pound. By signs the children let it be understood that they offered fifty roubles for a bar of chocolate and forty for a cigarette. The sailors could not believe their eyes and decided that these notes must be forged. But their comrades who'd already been there before contradicted them. It was the official black market rate in the White Sea and they must take advantage of it if they wanted any additional fun when they went ashore.

Trade began. The sailors threw down cigarettes and bars of chocolate. The children caught them with amazing skill and handed over the roubles by one of them climbing on the shoulders of another. In the excitement of bargaining, they made no attempt to cheat their customers. At one moment a sailor threw a tin of pilchards among them. The children scattered as if it had been a bomb. Having seen that the object was harmless, they left it lying there and began once more to shout and gesticulate.

None of them ate any of the chocolate or lit a cigarette. They put their treasures away, probably to barter later. Did they work on their own account, and if not for whom? Where did they get these bundles of roubles? None of the Allied sailors ever found out. As soon as the young speculators had exhausted their funds they disappeared almost as swiftly as they had come, and the wooden landing stages were deserted once more.

During the next two days, the ships sailed up to Archangel. From time to time along the flat shores they met antiquated paddle-steamers—rusty, dirty, strangely spectral ships loaded with wood or empty. Their crews of men and women passed with never a reply or a sign to the calls and waves of the Allied seamen.

At first sight Archangel did not seem unattractive with its long row of very modern houses dominated by the large green pagoda-like tower of the opera house. The nearer they approached the less seductive the town appeared. The quays as well as the streets, flanked with modern buildings, were particularly filthy and the stench was appalling. Although the inhabitants were not quite so ragged as the peasants they had seen so far, they were very poorly dressed. The first men to go ashore reported that the population was entirely composed of old people. The men and most of the women of combatant age had obviously left Archangel. This was not conducive to gaiety. All these pathetic old people in the street stared at the Allied sailors. They stared at them but never replied to their friendly greetings and moved away if they were offered a cigarette, although it was worth forty roubles.

Two restaurants, the Tourist Hotel and the International Club, were open to foreigners. A party of naval officers visited the Tourist Hotel on the first day. It was well kept and clean. On the tables were vases full of green grass for lack of flowers. The small orchestra alternately played Russian arias, such as the *Song of the Volga Boatmen,* or old blues. From time to time, the music was almost drowned by the blare of powerful loudspeakers in the street, " giving the latest war news," according to the head waiter. The Allied officers could order pink caviare, smoked salmon, crab, meat, butter and eggs and as much vodka as they liked. At the neighbouring tables Russian officers on leave ate with their wives. The couples seemed ill at ease and almost frigid. They threw rapid glances at the strangers and spoke little. With the help of the vodka the Allied officers soon forgot this restraint. The dinner cost them a hundred roubles a head, *i.e.* £5 at the official rate. But, since all the officers had asked their men to act as brokers the previous evening at Brevennik, they did not find the prices at the Tourist Hotel too exorbitant.

The liberty men could dine in the restaurant of the International Club (the Tourist was reserved for officers). The menus and the prices were very much the same. The International Club had a dance floor with hostesses exactly like those in Murmansk. The sailors were disappointed, as their comrades had been in the other ports, and they were soon wandering down the main street in search of souvenirs. All the shops were open and they could buy as they pleased, but their shelves were nearly empty. The following is a list of the most popular tourist items to be had in the Archangel shops at that time: small whalebone brooches, door bells, carnival masks, tweezers, wooden spoons, rattles and cheap bicycle bells. Nothing else—no clothes, shoes, linen or rugs—nothing except what has been enumerated. I am wrong. An officer, as a special favour and under the counter, obtained a dozen gramophone records in exchange for five cigarettes. He must have taken the records without knowing what they were. When he played them on his return to the ship, they were the Stalin speeches.

The men on shore leave, walking down the main street, were constantly approached by children, probably the same ones they had met in Brevennik, who whispered the same litany, furtively showing bundles of roubles like the sellers of filthy postcards in Port Said. They were usually chased away by women policemen in uniform with wide belts and pointed caps. The urchins took to their heels but returned a moment later.

Apart from its girl robots, the International Club possessed a cinema. They were showing " Every Dawn I Die."

The sailors also visited the opera, which was giving a comic opera ; it was completely incomprehensible but must have been very funny, to judge by the reactions of the Russian audience. Here at least they seemed to relax and even to be enjoying themselves. Only here could the visitors see that the inhabitants of Archangel still knew how to laugh.

In this port, as in Murmansk, parties were given by the officers of both fleets with the same ritual. Plenty of vodka and toasts. There were no incidents. The only relations between the Allies and the Russians were collective. Individual contacts were discouraged and even forbidden.

Their stay was more agreeable than that of their shipmates in Murmansk because there were no bombing attacks. Nevertheless, the crews soon felt depressed and homesick. There was no pleasure wandering round the empty shops or in the dirty unsavoury streets, full of old people who looked at them but never replied. They soon grew tired of the Russian food, of smoked salmon and vodka. They missed their beer. After a few days they did not even leave their ships and waited impatiently to set sail.

On the 23rd June, the bombers arrived in mass over Murmansk, obviously intent upon making a heavy raid. The Russian fighters engaged them as soon as the first bombs fell, but they were outnumbered. Waves of bombers came over in succession, each wave arriving as the previous one was diving on the target. The docks were a mass of flame and it seemed as though the port installations would never survive this attack. In actual fact, as often happens, the results were not too disastrous. Nevertheless the unloading of the last ships of PQ 16 had to be postponed. It was decided that the return convoy (QP 13) should set sail at once without waiting for the laggards. These were replaced by vessels of a previous convoy which had remained at Murmansk for the same reasons. Discontent was very high aboard the ships which had to remain. As they watched the gangs of men and women repairing the rails along the quay, the seamen in these ships wondered if another attack would destroy their work on the following day. Eventually, they began to grumble that their stay in Murmansk would only end in the destruction of their ship and in their own death. They were furious and almost in despair at being unable to leave this spot they had so eagerly desired to see appear on the horizon less than a month ago.

On the morning of the 26th June, a rumour ran round the crew of the unloaded cargo vessels that they were to sail on the following day. For some days the First Mates, wishing to conform to the recommendations as regards sailors' diet (not too much tinned foods and plenty of vitamins) had been doing their best to procure some fresh provisions for the return voyage. Unfortunately, the resources of Murmansk were as poor in this respect as they were in every other. The cooks were given potatoes and a few carcases of reindeer, which they looked upon with great suspicion. Reindeer meat proved to be quite eatable with a sauce but quite disgusting when roasted.

A new attack by dive bombers took place on the 27th at 03.00. Five hours later, sailing orders were confirmed for that evening. The convoy learned at the same time that the British minesweeper *H.M.S. Gossamer* (850 tons) had been sunk slightly higher up the river during the course of the morning attack. Thirteen killed. Their impatience to set sail grew more intense.

The ship whose company was by no means the most impatient but certainly the happiest to leave, was probably the British minesweeper *H.M.S. Niger*. The Captain had just received orders to join the convoy of QP 13. The *Niger* had not been at Murmansk for a month or two months or three months: she had spent the winter there. During those interminable months of the Arctic winter, in total or almost total darkness, the *Niger* had swept the magnetic mines dropped by aircraft in the river and the estuary, and broken the ice which blocked the channels. Her crew had been subjected to hundreds of bombing attacks (in nine days of April, 1942, 106 alerts). They had repelled numerous attacks against their own ship and they had been lucky enough not to be hit. Above all, they had endured eight months of exile which was almost in the nature of captivity. Now they would see their own country and their families in the hope that they would never be sent back to Murmansk. It would be someone else's turn. These men had learned patience. Far more than the crews of the other ships in PQ 16, they must have feared to see their ship destroyed on the blessed day of sailing. But now this day had come.

CHAPTER FIVE

The Tragedy of QP 13

THE CONVOY QP 13 SET SAIL FROM
Murmansk on the 27th June, 1942, at 17.00. A few hours
later it met the other ships which had sailed from Archangel to join it. The convoy now consisted of thirty-five
merchant ships with an escort of five British destroyers and
nine smaller warships—corvettes, sloops and minesweepers.
Most of the cargo vessels sailed in ballast.

The QP 13's orders were to sail N.N.E. in the direction
of Novaya Zemlya, then to change course for the Franz
Josef Archipelago. In fact, to go as far north as possible
and to skirt the summer icepack. At the cost of this big
detour it would have a chance of escaping the aircraft.

The sailors thought that their best chance at the moment
lay in the bad visibility, in this foggy weather which seemed
to have set in. Were it only to last a few days, only five
days, they would get through.

At midday on the 30th June, the convoy reached the
position 74° 24′ N. Beyond that lay the ice. The QP 13
began to skirt it in a westerly direction. A reassuring
feature: the fog persisted despite the intense cold. This
really gave the impression of Polar navigation. The little
open space in the milky ocean was dotted with floebergs.
On account of these progress was slow. A few of the Captains in the starboard column, thinking they were skirting
an ice floe, found their ships in channels of the ice pack ;
finding themselves without issue or being lost in a veritable
maze, they had to reverse with engines astern, trembling
for their screw and sending a motor launch to push aside

the ice blocks. This was often a great strain on the Captains and the crews. However, it was better than being attacked by German aircraft.

On the 30th June, about 17.00, the fog disappeared to the south. A big twin-engined plane was seen in the distance low on the horizon but easily identifiable. With dismay the men saw it and many of them smiled bitterly. The plane was flying east and did not deviate its course. It did not seem to have seen the convoy. The men breathed again. A quarter of an hour later the wireless operators of the escort vessels decoded this message from the Admiralty: "You have probably been spotted by enemy aircraft."

QP 13 had not in fact been spotted. During this voyage it was neither to be spotted nor attacked by aircraft: another fate awaited it. The fog in which it had been shrouded almost since leaving Murmansk would continue to protect it for more than a week, until the morning of 5th July. The weather remained unchanged: a calm sea and bitterly cold. The ships had become once more heavy icy spectres, moaning in the fog. Below decks, in the messes, stations and cabins, the damp trickled. The men suffered from this oozing damp and from the cold when they had to remain for half an hour on deck. But anything was better than aircraft.

Several wireless operators caught transmissions from U-boats hunting in those waters. The sharks were looking for their prey. But they were mechanical sharks without hunting instinct or scent and they no longer had "that vile bat" to guide them.

It is not quite true to say that the fog persisted without a break until the 5th July: on the 2nd July it lifted for a short time. QP 13 could see smoke fifteen miles north on the horizon. These funnels belonged to the seventy ships of the convoy PQ 17. This convoy was on its way to Murmansk and two-thirds of its ships would never reach port. We shall describe its tragic odyssey later.

On the morning of 5th July, the Captain D and the Commodore of the QP 13 received the following message from the Admiralty: " Eleven German warships have put to sea from their bases in the fjords. Last reported at 71° 31′ N., 27° 10′ E."

A little later the weather changed. A stiff breeze sprang up which dispersed the fog and whipped up the sea.

The breeze stiffened during the day. At 20.00, as the officers left their watch, they noted in their navigating logs: " State of the sea 7." This meant that quite a gale was blowing. The ships sailing in ballast were tossed about like corks and the waves broke over the decks. The convoy had descended in latitude and the uninterrupted daylight was replaced by a greyish light which heralded the return of night. Now, when it should have been sailing at the greatest possible speed in view of the threat reported in the Admiralty's signal, QP 13 ploughed its way slowly in the rough sea.

The duty fit survivors of convoy PQ 16 had been split up for the return journey (QP 13) among the vessels which had lost men either at sea or at Murmansk. Thus our greaser, Shorty, a survivor from *The City of Joliet,* was now aboard the American cargo vessel *John Randolph.*

Work in the engine room is particularly unpleasant in bad weather. Although he no longer suffered from seasickness, as he had done during his first years at sea, Shorty felt uncomfortable in a rough sea, perhaps because of his bad liver. He found his hours on watch in the engine room very long on that 5th of July. The deck rose and fell, swinging in all directions like a crazy lift. The ram blows of the water made the hull shiver. The smell of fuel, grease and steam made him feel sick.

Shorty had been on watch from midnight to four o'clock, then from 12.00 to 16.00, and then the dog watch 18.00 till 20.00. He was on watch again from 08.00 till 12.00. At

20.00 on the 5th July, he left the engine room, rinsed his face and hands and lay down on his bunk, fully dressed.

He had eaten a snack at teatime, and it was enough to see the mess at this hour to realise that it would have been ridiculous to try and sit down at a table in front of a plate. Moreover, he merely felt an animal desire to go and have a sleep, if that were possible. Shorty knew that the wind had blown away the fog, but he knew nothing of the Admiralty signal. In this weather he did not think there was much chance of enemy planes appearing. The U-boats, without their recco planes, were hardly to be feared. This storm was almost as good as the fog it represented.

But Shorty did not fall asleep. All the men in the Arctic convoys, although lying in their bunks, could not help keeping an ear on the alert. It was often a long time before sleep put an end to their anxieties.

Shorty looked at his watch: 20.35. He closed his eyes. A few minutes later two dull explosions made him jump. With beating heart he sat up in his bunk. The alarm bells were ringing. He was already on his feet, putting on his boots and life-jacket. He climbed the iron ladder, still struggling into his suit, jostled by the others who were also running to their action stations. And then he was on deck.

On all sides sprays of foam rose from the sea with dull roars. In the greyish twilight he could see ships listing in all directions on the livid waves while around them these geysers spurted one after the other. The men were paralysed with fright. No gun had fired and all they could hear was the roar of the explosions. Shorty distinctly saw a geyser raise the sea just beneath a vessel, which immediately took on a heavy list to stern. Another waterspout 200 yards ahead of the *John Randolph* and another 100 yards on the port bow. They might have been witnessing a revolt of the sea, a ruthless aggression on the part of a sea determined to engulf the whole convoy. The men started shouting, wondering what had happened, and swearing because their guns were not firing. But no enemy was visible, neither on the sea nor in the grey ragged sky. A signal was flown at the Commodore's masthead, ordering a change of course.

A man running down from the bridge cried: "They're torpedoes or mines." At that moment a small escort vessel rocked by an explosion, sank. It was the minesweeper *H.M.S. Niger,* whose crew had been so happy to be setting out for home after eight months spent at Murmansk. The corvette *Roselys* picked up three survivors from a crew of 150.

The cargo ship which had been hit had just sunk. An escort vessel sped towards its boats in which the crew were huddled.

The men of the *John Randolph* saw cannon fire to port. Some ships were firing but no one knew the nature of the target. The geysers continued to spout on all sides. This absence of any visible enemy was more terrifying than any other form of attack. They felt they had been caught in a deadly trap with no hope of escape. Other guns had started to fire, but still no one knew what at.

The explosions must have hit the *John Randolph* just abaft the beam. The men felt the shock—an enormous shudder which made the whole ship rock. She began to sink at once and the Captain gave orders to abandon ship.

Shorty found himself surrounded by a host of shouting, running, jostling men. He saw the boat ahead of him on a level with the guardrail. He climbed over and jumped in. He fell on his knees in the boat, scraping his shins. Then he felt himself precipitated to the stern of the boat, as it dived almost vertically, and he fell into the sea. A false manoeuvre had paid out the rope too soon from one of the davits.

He thought that he was drowning, until he realised that he was floating to the surface, thanks to the buoyancy of his life-jacket. But the rise seemed to last an eternity.

He was suffocating but at last he came to the surface. His heart was beating furiously.

The side of the *John Randolph* was there, a few feet away. He began to swim away from it. He felt the icy water on his face and hands. The rollers made swimming almost impossible for the crests of the waves broke and engulfed him.

Suddenly he saw a raft close to the *John Randolph*. It was rising and falling impressively along the hull. Shorty realised that the waves were bearing him towards the raft, so he put up no resistance. In any case he could not have swum against them. A few seconds later he was clutching the raft.

He remained for a moment with his body in the sea, still hanging on, following the rise and fall. He was in a dangerous position, for it kept turning, and he risked finding himself crushed between the raft and the hull. Then he saw other shipwrecked men hanging on like him and hoisting themselves on to the raft. Their dank hair hung down their foreheads and their faces were as white as chalk. They hoisted themselves up and lay there flat and motionless, clutching on to the planking of the raft. Several were already aboard. Shorty shouted for them to help him up, but no one moved. Perhaps they had not heard him. Then he summoned all his energy. Kicking violently, he pulled on his arms and contracted his muscles. At last he got one knee up and the rest was easy. Shorty was lying on his belly like the others, hanging on for grim death.

The raft rose and fell with the waves. It now tended to leave the hull, but the pendants which had not been slipped held it back. One of the men took out his knife and cut one of the ropes. The other broke. Shorty saw it rise in the air like a whiplash. The raft nearly capsized and the men screamed, but it righted itself. It rose and fell with the waves, sometimes washed by the crests.

The *John Randolph* was still afloat, although she was

three-quarters below the waves. Two of her boats drew away. They could see the men rowing in the heavy seas. The ship now seemed at least fifty yards away, but it was difficult from their level to estimate distance. Shorty, of course, like the rest of them was still overwhelmed by the tragedy. He found that this shipwreck was infinitely more dramatic than that of *The City of Joliet*.

The men on the raft felt a shock, followed by an enormous submarine vibration ; then they heard the dull sound of an explosion. No one said a word but they must all have been thinking like Shorty: a near explosion could kill them all or wreck the raft. So far, Shorty had had no time to think of this danger, or to notice that all the guns had stopped firing. He thought now that the *John Randolph* and the other ships must have been blown up by the mines.

The *John Randolph* was still sinking slowly. Her empty deck was now awash. The vision of the men on the raft was very limited. They could only see the superstructure of their ship, the two lifeboats a little further off and occasionally, on the top of a wave, two other cargo vessels, sailing away.

After an indeterminate space of time they ceased to see these ships. Fortunately, the submarine explosions seemed to have ceased, but the shipwrecked men felt abandoned in this raging sea with the two boats and the wreck of the *John Randolph*. Then the ship disappeared completely and nothing remained but the two boats, which also seemed to be drawing away from them.

Corpses in life-jackets or lifebelts float upright or almost upright with their faces in the water. Other drowned men begin by floating stretched full length or slightly on a slant just below the surface with their backs just appearing. When Shorty saw the first dead man a few yards from the raft—several together in their bright orange life-jackets— he did not immediately realise that they were corpses. At first he thought that they would catch on to the raft and try to clamber aboard. There will be too many of us, he thought, and the raft will not bear the weight. But then in a flash he understood.

The men, upright in the sea, drifted towards the raft, peacefully following the movement of the waves, head bent forward and their hair floating like seaweed from their foreheads. They had no interest in the raft, for they could not see. They were drifting in another world, and now they were unrecognizable strangers even for those who could have recognized their faces dipping in the waves. Some of them must have been killed by the explosion or asphyxiated, as Shorty had been afraid of being in the water.

And now he saw others without their life-saving kit. They must have perished of cold after a few minutes in this freezing water, or been drowned as sailors were in the good old days.

Shorty's companions had begun to speak. He heard some of them groaning at the sight of the corpses. The raft rose and fell and the dead bodies drifted towards them until one of them, raised by a wave, almost landed on the raft. At this the living men groaned and cried even louder, as though the contact with this poor dead man, their former shipmate, threatened to carry them into the beyond.

The school of corpses haunted the raft for some time but finally only a few remained. At least one was usually visible on the little expanse of dark foaming sea in the grey twilight which in the Arctic takes the place of night.

All the shipwrecked men on the raft—as far as Shorty remembers there were seven or eight—were wearing their life-saving suits. This garment gave complete protection to their body but not to their hands which were constantly plunged in the icy water. The wind formed ice on their faces until they had no feeling. The men could only feel their eyes which throbbed and burnt from the oil-polluted sea water. A sailor next to Shorty was suffering from seasickness. He twisted and turned, vomiting bile. It was obvious that he would not last long.

The groans and murmurs lasted some time after the passage of the school of corpses and had then ceased. Now Shorty only heard the infernal whistle of the wind which rose and fell with the movement of the raft—loud when they were in a trough, shrill and spasmodic when they were on the crest of the wave. After a time he ceased to hear the straining of the man who was seasick. He was certain that he had disappeared, but he did not look in his direction. He moved his hands from time to time to assure himself that he could still feel them.

Shorty was certain that he had not slept or fainted for in that case he would certainly have lost hold. At one moment, however, he thought he must have come out of a long sleep. Around him the men were talking and shouting because of the wind. Shorty saw a long red serpent falling in the sky and heard an explosion.

The slow descent of the red serpent over the dark sea in this sinister twilight was inevitably eerie. It seemed like a cosmic or a supernatural phenomena, a terrible sight from heaven. At first they were all terrified. One of them muttered the word "Aircraft," while others maintained that they were German planes coming to bomb them and to rake them with machine-gun fire. These survivors were already exhausted by their long period of immobility, clutching to the raft in this raging sea and howling wind.

Other luminous serpents fell from the sky and other explosions were heard. At last one of the men said that they were boats firing flares to denote their presence. This was the correct explanation. Some shipwrecked men in their boats had noticed the escort vessels which had remained near the wrecks or had returned, and for fear of not being seen in this sombre half-light had fired flares. Most of the lifeboats contained signalling material as well as provisions.

Shorty and his companions could not see the lifeboats for their horizon was too limited. But as soon as they grasped the meaning of these flares they realized that they were not abandoned as they had thought, and hope was reborn. They all began to talk at once and to offer all manner of suggestions.

As soon as hope rose the shipwrecked men (apart from those who had already died of exhaustion) began to speak with a volubility which no one can imagine unless he had had a similar personal experience. In a few seconds they passed from hope to despair and once more to hope, thinking out rational or the craziest solutions.

As soon as Shorty and his companions from the top of a wave saw the black shapes of the rescue ships—(" There are two, not three! No—one! " In actual fact there were three)—they nearly all began to shout at the top of their voices as though the ship could have heard them in this wind which took their breath away. Then, becoming reasonable, they told each other that these ships would soon spot them. They encouraged those who remained silent, probably from exhaustion. They must stick it out at all costs.

This period of waiting was a nightmare. And yet at one moment the ships (now they saw that there were three) seemed quite near and then they felt that they were further away and had grown quite small. None of these men were in a state to have an objective vision. The half-light, the movements of their craft, and the tall rollers which hid everything from view, added to their uncertainty.

And yet the presence of the ships became more and more a fact and more and more permanent. The more optimistic who already saw themselves saved, began to talk of their plans, still shouting because of the wind. They would never go to sea again, this profession was finished for them for ever. One of them insisted that if he were taken to Iceland, which was obviously the nearest land, he would refuse to leave the island until the end of the war. Others approved most vehemently. Yes, they would refuse to leave Iceland whatever happened to them. They would rather go to gaol. If the worst came to the worst they would commit crimes to get put in gaol if anyone tried to put them on a ship before the end of the war. They made a joint resolution to this effect.

The rescue vessel, a sloop, was now really close at hand. They could see her heavy silhouette rising and falling. Alongside was a lifeboat, as light as a feather. Each time the boat touched the hull, men caught hold of the large net and the crew of the sloop helped them aboard. It must have been quite near for all these details to be visible from the raft. From the bows of the sloop other sailors looked down at the raft and waved from time to time. Shorty and his companions shouted, raised their heads and hoisted themselves up on their elbows. Shorty was trembling. He could no longer feel his hands.

The sloop got into position and the men on the raft could now only see its massive bows and the funnel above them. It was making for them and manoeuvring to draw closer to the raft, and to approach on the side where the net hung. The English sailors looked down at the ship-wrecked men with great compassion. They seemed very efficient.

Suddenly the men on the raft changed position and it capsized. Shorty thought once more that he was drowned. But no, he was still on the raft and he had even banged his head on it. He tried to catch hold of the edge but it was impossible. His hands were completely lifeless. Then he made a great effort to swim as far as the sloop and after a few strokes he touched the hull. He put one arm in a huge mesh and then the other. Since he could not use his hands he used his arms like a man whose hands had been cut off. He saw two other shipwrecked men in the sea not far away beyond the raft. The sailors in the sloop had thrown lines to them but they could not catch hold of them and were carried away by the waves. Raising his head,

Shorty saw the head and shoulders of other sailors speaking to him and telling him to hoist himself up. He shook his head and looked up with a piteous face. Then two of them climbed over the rail and descended the net. He felt himself seized by the shoulders. A moment later Shorty was lying in sick bay among other survivors. The sailors gave him something hot to drink. He still could not feel his hands. His eyes smarted, one of his feet was very painful and even the cup burnt his lips—but what did that matter! The sick-bay, shaken by the big rollers, was sweating with damp ; it was full of men lying there, boots and clothes in disorder, but it was a marvellous haven—an incomparable palace. And Shorty's life which had been saved, the life of the wretched greaser Shorty with no family, nothing and no one in the world, was a precious and irreplaceable life, a refound treasure.

In all probability, the Commodore of Convoy QP 13 had made a bad landfall. In other words, blinded by a fog of several days duration, he had made an error in his navigation and the convoy had entered the minefield laid by the British to bar the Denmark Strait which separates Iceland from Greenland.

Several ships, thinking that it was an attack by surface warships, U-boats or E-boats, had opened fire. The gunners had fired at random and it was lucky that they had not hit each other.

As soon as the Commodore ordered a change of course, the convoy turned south. The corvette *Roselys* and the armed sloops *St. Elstan* and *Lady Madeleine* patrolled until two in the morning to pick up the survivors. It was a heavy sea, strength seven to eight, a north-easterly wind, force seven, visibility half a mile. The vessels signalled their presence by flares or blinking red lamps. Lifeless bodies were drifting in the water. They left them in favour of those who were still alive.

An officer of the *Roselys* witnessed the most terrible

scenes: "A man to whom we had thrown a line which he tried to seize with his numbed fingers, sank just as we were going to rescue him. Three of the men in a big metal sloop who, in spite of our warnings, tried to jump aboard when the winch had brought them on a level with us, missed their footing and the following wave crushed them to pulp between the two hulls. I literally heard heads crushed like nuts. I was violently sick."

The *Roselys* sailed up and down in this raging sea, drawing alongside the boats and rafts, picking up isolated shipwrecked men. She was full of survivors. They were everywhere, in the offices, in the mess, the cabins and the engine rooms. The corvette continued with her human fishing until she was certain that on the scene of the tragedy there were only empty boats and deserted rafts. By this time it was two o'clock. The *Roselys* set a southerly course to get out of the minefield, then turned S.S.E. and joined the *Lady Madeleine* and the *St. Elstan*. There were forty survivors on board the former and twenty-seven on the latter. On board the *Roselys*,[1] 179. The three ships arrived that afternoon at Reykjavik, each with its flag at half-mast.

Five ships of the convoy QP 13 were blown up by mines and sank on the night of the 6/7th July, 1942. The *John Randolph, The Heffron,* the *Heibert,* the *Massmar,* the *Rodina* (Russian cargo vessel) and the British minesweeper *H.M.S. Niger.*

---

[1] A few days later, when his ship reached Argentia, the American Naval Base in Newfoundland, the Captain of the *Roselys* received from Vice-Admiral Braynard, O.C. Task Force 24 (American Atlantic Fleet), an official letter in which the Admiral said, among other things: "Five young officers of the American Mercantile Marine. survivors from ships sunk in the convoy QP 13, have been questioned during their stay at Argentia on the events of which they were witness . . . without exception they expressed the greatest admiration and gratitude for the skill you showed in saving the survivors and for the seaman-like and efficient organisation aboard your vessel in the treatment and care given to the survivors. They all state, without reserve, that they owe their lives to your superb seamanship and to the efficiency of the men under your command. You deserve to be congratulated. You and the men under your command have earned the respect and gratitude of the United States Navy."

Among the victims were the wife and two children of the Soviet Naval Attaché in London. Their bodies were seen in the water but it was impossible to save them.

CHAPTER SIX

PQ 17—The Massacred Convoy

CONVOY PQ 17 FORMED DURING JUNE, 1942, consisted of thirty-three merchant ships, three rescue ships and a naval tanker. Twenty-two of the cargo vessels were American. Several of them had already accomplished the Murmansk Run.

The escort consisted of six destroyers, two flak-ships (large converted cargo boats with powerful anti-aircraft armament), two submarines, eleven corvettes, plus a dozen minesweepers and armed sloops. Moreover, the PQ 17 was to be protected by important support and cover forces as will be seen.

The German Command was informed by its spies of the composition of the convoy and the proposed date of sailing (27th June from Iceland).

In every country at war the composition of convoys and sailing dates are, in theory, top secrets. Even the captains are only informed at the last moment. And yet the naval authorities are obliged to give the captains orders in advance concerning the loading of their vessels, their provisioning and fuel. I am not insinuating for one moment that any of these captains chattered irresponsibly. Without exception they were fully aware of their responsibility. They know that if their secrets were learned by the enemy it might entail the loss of their ship, the death of their men and themselves. But they could not carry out their orders regarding loading and provisioning in absolute secret. The sailors were present at these operations and even carried them out. They, too, did not desire their own death or the death of their comrades. But how can one expect a secret shared by several thousand men to be rigorously kept? The enemy agents did not wander in black cloaks round the basins, casting an inquisitive eye on the ships. They simply haunted the pubs and had only to be cordial and hospitable.

Receiving information then, of the composition and sailing dates of convoy PQ 17, the German Naval Command decided to despatch a force to destroy it consisting of the 35,000-ton battleship *Tirpitz*, the 10,000-ton pocket battleship *Admiral Scheer,* the 10,000-ton heavy cruiser *Admiral Hipper* and seven destroyers.

The Allied Naval Command at this period did not know the exact composition of this attacking force. It was, however, aware of the importance of the German Naval forces stationed in the fjords and certain movements allowed it to suspect that the irruption they had always feared of the German battleships on the convoy route was imminent. As a result the two following squadrons were detailed to protect convoy PQ 17.

The " Support Force " under the orders of Vice-Admiral L. H. K. Hamilton: the British cruisers *H.M.S. London* (flagship) and *H.M.S. Norfolk ;* the heavy American cruisers *Wichita* and *Tuscalousa ;* nine destroyers and corvettes. The main duty of this force was to intercept enemy aircraft and U-boats making their way towards the convoy.

The " Covering Force," under the orders of Admiral Sir Jack Tovey, C.-in-C. Home Fleet: the 35,000-ton battleship *H.M.S. Duke of York* (flagship), the 35,000-ton American battleship *Washington* (in which Rear-Admiral Giffen flew his flag), the 23,000-ton aircraft carrier *H.M.S. Victorious,* the British cruisers *H.M.S. Cumberland, H.M.S. Nigeria* and *H.M.S. Manchester ;* a dozen destroyers and corvettes. The mission of this force was to cruise in the Arctic Ocean and the North Atlantic during the crossing of the PQ 17 and, if necessary, to intercept the German squadron.

In fact the protectors of convoy PQ 17 (in all two 35,000-

ton battleships, an aircraft carrier, seven cruisers, a score of destroyers, two submarines, a score of corvettes and sloops) were nearly twice as numerous as the merchant vessels they had to protect.

The route of the convoy had been planned as follows: it was to hug the west and north coast of Iceland as far as longitude 19° ; to sail N.E. as far as latitude 75° N., skirting the coast of Jan Mayen Island ; from there due east until it had passed Bear Island. Then another change of course to the south-east and finally south to the mouth of the White Sea.

The convoy set sail from Hvalfjordur roads near Reykjavik on the 27th June. The " covering force " set sail from Scapa Flow on the 29th June ; the " support force " from Seidisfjord, Iceland, on the 1st July.

In the Denmark Strait the convoy ran into a thick fog and had to sail slowly on a sea encumbered with many large ice floes. The fog, as we know, meant no aircraft. It was not until 1st July when the convoy had reached a point two hundred miles west of the Bear Island that the first German " recco " aircraft appeared. One of the planes was injudicious enough to come too near and was shot down by ack-ack.

An effort had been made to give the PQ 17 an anti-aircraft armament slightly less inadequate than that carried by the preceding convoys. Some of the ships were decently armed, others not. On board the Panamanian cargo ship *Troubadour* (flying the Panamanian flag which was in reality the American flag), Reserve Ensign H. E. Caraway commanding the naval armed guard conceived a simple and rather ingenious idea. With the Captain's consent he removed the crates from the two tanks being carried on deck, assembled their 37 mm cannon and brought up ammunition from the hold. These cannon were used in the course of the 4th July attack and one German aircraft was shot down. Caraway was apparently congratulated for his initiative, but to my surprise I have never read that this ingenious precedent was used anywhere else than in the *Troubadour*.

The Germans, as I have already mentioned, knew the composition and the sailing date of PQ 17. They do not seem to have been informed in advance of the support and covering forces. The former was spotted and reported by a German submarine at sixty miles east of Jan Mayen Island. The naval command at Narvik immediately despatched aircraft which returned to base with inaccurate reports. In these accounts the cruiser *H.M.S. London* was promoted to the rank of battleship and the cruisers *Wichita* and *Tuscalousa* were given as aircraft carriers. The fog was the obvious reason for these mistakes. Moreover, the airmen had spotted the convoy QP 13 in the same zone. Now the protection of a home-bound convoy consisting of almost empty ships did not justify the use of a battleship and two aircraft carriers. The Germans were perplexed and even worried.

Radio-telegraphic messages began to circulate between Narvik and Berlin and between Berlin and the short-wave sets of German spies in Great Britain and Iceland.

Convoy PQ 17 was subjected to attack by U-boats, torpedo-carrying aircraft and dive bombers on the 2nd, 3rd and 4th July, 1942—to be more precise during those three days of perpetual daylight. The evidence of the attacks increased until the sensational incident which occurred on the 4th July about 20.00.

Six submarines (the number is in doubt) opened the attacks on the early morning of the 2nd. They were spotted by the destroyers and the escort corvettes which attacked them with depth charges before they could approach the convoy close enough to fire. These assailants apparently did not push home their attack. The information about this attack is vague.

A few hours later the Commodore and Captain D. of PQ 17 received the following message from the Admiralty:

"The Admiralty in agreement with the Admiral commanding the Allied naval forces in North Russia considers that it would be ill-advised to try and unload the cargoes at Murmansk. They are to proceed to Archangel."

Without any other comment. It was easy to realise that the Germans must be heavily bombing the Soviet port. The German High Command seemed determined to stop material reinforcements being sent to Russia by the Arctic route.

Eight torpedo bombers attacked the convoy on the afternoon of the same day, 2nd July, but they obtained no more results than the submarines had done and one was shot down.

On the 3rd July, PQ 17 and its escort changed on to their easterly course. The captains of the warships received two more messages from the British Admiralty. The first announced the total destruction of Murmansk by the Luftwaffe. It was inspired by information which turned out to be exceedingly pessimistic. The damage caused by bombing attacks is often over-estimated on first sight. It was, however, true that Murmansk was being subjected to extremely heavy and almost uninterrupted bombing, causing great destruction. Fires ravaged the town, the railway station and the quays.

The second message ran: "The *Tirpitz,* the *Hipper* and four destroyers have left Trondhjem."

The contents of neither of these two telegrams were communicated to the merchant ships.

The same day, the 3rd July, twenty-six dive bombers arrived at 15.00 from the south. They were certainly hampered by the low cloud above the convoy. Instead of choosing their targets from altitude and diving directly upon them like birds of prey, they had to dive very obliquely, hesitating, taking avoiding action while the gunners, encouraged by their recent success, fired with calm and resolution. In short, the twenty-six dive bombers had to retire without having registered a single hit. The attack ended with a new defensive victory for PQ 17. The convoy kept its regular formation according to schedule without having suffered a single loss.

The weather cleared. Towards the end of the afternoon smoke appeared on the horizon to the north. Then the powerful shapes of vessels rose above the clear-cut line. There were a few rather anxious moments before the crews were reassured by seeing these arrivals exchange signals with the Captain D. They were the cruisers of the supporting force.

These warships did not approach any nearer to the convoy. They began to patrol almost parallel to its route, just within sight. The crews of PQ 17 would have liked to see these protectors on their starboard beam from which all the air attacks arrived. But the supporting force remained north of the convoy, always in sight (official commentators speak of the reassuring sight of this force) but too far to bring aid from its powerful anti-aircraft artillery. I have nowhere found a true and satisfactory explanation for this behaviour. We shall soon see that this was not to remain the only obscure point in the behaviour of the Allied naval forces during the next few days. Five attacks took place on the 4th July.

The first at 03.00 was launched by a single Heinkel 115 torpedo bomber which emerged from a bank of fog to starboard. Its torpedo passed between the *Samuel Chase* and the *Carlton* and made for the liberty ship *Christopher Newport*. The Reserve ensign in command of the naval armed guard ordered his men to fire the 30 mm machine-gun at the torpedo whose wake was quite visible. The gun loaders panicked, rushed down the companionway of the spar deck and made for the boats, shouting to the gun captain, a leading seaman named Hugh P. Wright, to follow them. Instead of doing so, Wright opened fire at the nose of the torpedo. He continued to fire until the air bubbles had disappeared beneath the boats which the others had already begun to fill. The explosion hurled him two decks lower on to the embarkation deck. He sprained his ankle and fainted. The torpedo hit the *Christopher Newport* in the engine room. She had to be abandoned and was sunk by one of the escorting submarines.

Thus the first victim was an American ship. The sailors in the British vessels, both merchant and naval, could not fail to establish some relation between cause and effect when a few moments later they saw all the American ships strike their flag. This meant but one thing: surrender. Now one could not reasonably suppose that all the American ships in the convoy should have decided to surrender because one of theirs had been sunk. And surrender to whom? The British did not understand. From all their bridges binoculars were levelled on the American ships. The watchers then saw these ships in unison hoisting in the place of the dirty frayed flag they had hauled down, the national stars and stripes which seemed double as large on account of its vivid colours. One of the spectators immediately realised the truth and soon they all understood. It was the 4th July—Independence Day. The American citizens were commemorating among their British shipmates the anniversary of the day their country had flung off the yoke of British domination. The descendants of the oppressors and the oppressed of old now risked their wealth and life together in the struggle against another powerful oppressor. We could discuss this at some length but it is not the purpose of this book. I have merely given the reasons why none of the American survivors of PQ 17 would ever confuse this 1942 Independence Day with any other.

At 04.00 on the 4th July, the convoy had therefore lost only one ship. At this juncture the Commodore and the escort leader received another telegram from the Admiralty. Here is the text:

" Aerial photographic reconnaissances confirm that none of the big German units is now in Trondhjem. The Admiralty considers that:

(a) A movement of the big German units is in progress towards the north.

(b) This movement constitutes a threat to the convoy but there is no indication of imminent danger.

(c) The weather is favourable for the progress of the convoy eastwards.

" In consequence the Admiralty is taking no action for the moment but is following developments."

This message was not communicated to the merchant ships any more than the preceding ones had been.

The convoy was now sailing beneath a ceiling of low cloud (300 - 500 feet) over a sea with a gentle swell. Between the sea and the layer of cloud the air gradually grew lighter.

The hour of the second attack on the 4th July has remained undetermined, as well as the number of the attackers. They were once more Heinkel 115s, but this time they attacked with bombs. They obtained no results and three of them were shot down. The gunners of PQ 17 were gaining confidence in themselves and the efforts to better the ships' armament had borne fruit.

The Commandants of the German bases in Norway were well aware of this. The reports of the airmen returning from ops informed them that PQ 17 was defending itself to good effect. But since they had received orders to harrass and annihilate this convoy they sent up a wave of twenty-five torpedo-carrying Focke-Wulfs.

These attacked the convoy about 13.15. It was during this action that the American destroyer *Wainwright* (Commander Moon) began to distinguish herself. The *Wainwright*, which was refuelling from the tanker *Aldersdale*, interrupted the operation to fight the attackers to starboard of the convoy. On its own it repelled six, but the others, despite the joint fire of the merchant ships and escorts, flew in close enough to launch at a good distance. Four cargo vessels were hit by torpedoes and fell astern. Two of them would later rejoin the convoy.

The supporting force still continued to sail north of the convoy.

The proof that the returning German aircraft had furnished remarkably accurate reports was to be given in an incontestable manner. The following attack was directed exclusively against the *Wainwright*.

Dive bombers attacked her successively from 17.00 onwards without bothering about the other ships. The aircraft came out of the cloud at 500 feet and dived on her. The little destroyer zig-zagged about the sea at full speed without ceasing to fire. The sailors in the other ships could see the geysers spurting all around her in the water. The *Wainwright* manoeuvred between these waterspouts. When calm returned and she had not been hit a single time, the rest of the convoy cheered. The destroyer sailed off proudly to take up her place against the head of the convoy.

At 18.20 a new formation of aircraft appeared on the horizon to the south, flying at low level. These machines seemed to be making for the centre of the starboard column. But at about 10,000 yards the formation of twenty-five Heinkel 111 torpedo bombers split in two. Half of them in line abreast continued towards the convoy while the others made for the *Wainwright*, enemy No. 1.

Captain Moon had lost nothing of his offensive spirit. He raced his destroyer at $33\frac{1}{2}$ knots towards the attackers with the intention of attacking them before they reached the launching position. He opened fire at 8,000 yards.

The line abreast formation began to waver. The other ships opened fire. Several aircraft were hit and others jettisoned their bombs. But the second half of the formation, primarily directed against the *Wainwright,* now attacked the convoy. Around and above the ships the air was filled with ack-ack bursts and criss-crossing tracers. The smooth scars of the torpedoes spread out at full speed on the water. The cargo ships took avoiding action in all directions. Some shaken by an explosion stopped and listed in a cloud of steam. The destroyers, their bows in the foam, listed beneath the effect of these fantastic gyrations and escaped these death-dealing tracks. Unable to torpedo the *Wainwright,* the enemy aircraft before leaving flew backwards and forwards over her, raking her with machine-guns. She was still untouched but several of her crew were wounded.

The attack ended at 18.30: it had lasted ten minutes. The liberty ship *William Hooper,* the tankers *Aldersdale* and *Azerbaijan,* all damaged, remained behind the convoy. The two first named were sunk by the escort. The *Azerbaijan,* considered as lost, was abandoned by her crew which had survived the explosion of the torpedo. Half an hour later the smoke which enveloped her dispersed. She was still afloat. The Captain in his boat called for volunteers to return aboard. The men succeeded in repairing the engines and getting the ship under way. She finally arrived at Archangel.

The balance sheet after this attack was as follows: Three ships sunk, six enemy aircraft shot down. The convoy at this moment was 240 miles from the North Cape, almost on the meridian of this Cape (precisely 240 miles to the north of Cape North). The ships still had more than 1,000 miles to sail before reaching Archangel. In other words, a five days run.

Here is the text of messages sent by the Admiralty on the 4th July, 1942, from 20.00 to the Commodore of the PQ 17 and the Commanders of the warships protecting the convoy.

First telegram: " Owing to threat from enemy surface forces, convoy is to disperse and proceed to Russian ports." Half an hour later: " Convoy will spread out." Half an hour later: " Cruisers will retire westward at full speed." A few moments later the senior British destroyer *H.M.S. Keppel,* flashed to all the escorts as well as to the merchant ships the following message: " Convoy scatter and proceed to Russian ports. Escorts, negative destroyers, proceed independently to Archangel."

It is hardly necessary to add that this message was a staggering blow to all its recipients.

Naturally, a report of the Sea Lords' deliberations, even had there been one, was never published. Historians and commentators have interpreted in various ways the decisions taken as a result of these deliberations.

The Admiralty *a priori* had no reason to fear an encounter between the attacking force *Tirpitz-Hipper* and the combined units of the support and covering forces. The balance was indisputably in favour of the Allies. But when one looks into the situation more closely, one discovers the following fact: On 4th July, 1942, at 20.00, the convoy PQ 17 had reached a position where in the case of an encounter, the German land-based aircraft could have intervened in greater numbers than the aircraft of *H.M.S. Victorious*.

The R.A.F. based on land could not at that period intervene at this distance in strength. (On the other hand, the powerful cover force on the 4th July at 20.00 was west of Spitzbergen 230 miles from the convoy, 400 miles from Altenfjord, which according to information the German warships had just left after provisioning, or were on the point of leaving. That is to say, it was too far away to help the PQ 17 before the irruption of the *Tirpitz* squadron. The decision to renounce exposing the whole fleet convoy-escort-cruisers to the formidable big guns of the *Tirpitz* and to prefer the scattering of the convoy and the withdrawal of the cruisers can therefore be defended. What remains obscure (apart from the obstinacy of the support force in keeping north of the convoy) is the behaviour of the cover force since it had set sail—a behaviour which was to result in the position of impotence mentioned above.

To recapitulate what has been said about the convoy PQ 16, which was also abandoned by its cruisers at a certain point, it is reasonable to suppose that the Admiralty was prepared to engage the *Tirpitz* squadron provided the encounter took place beyond the range of German aircraft or in a spot where it could only interfere weakly. To envisage an encounter in a more remote place was bound to pose the delicate problem of knowing whether it was right to expose dangerously (because of enemy air superiority) in the defence of precious cargoes, warships which were even more precious, perhaps indispensable, for operations decisive to the war.

Some British commentators have put forward this hypothesis:

The Admiralty may have feared that eventually the *Tirpitz* squadron would not sail north but west. Now, to let these formidable pirates escape into the Atlantic was to risk pursuing them for months, and in order to encompass their destruction to provide the convoys so vital to the United States-Great Britain with enormous escorts. The covering force, therefore, had to manoeuvre solely to prevent the *Tirpitz* squadron having access to the Atlantic. This meant that the cruisers also had to retire to cover the battleships and the aircraft carrier. And the cruisers themselves had to be covered by a screen of destroyers.

Many of the British sailors found it hard to carry out their Admiralty orders, which implied the sacrifice of the convoy. Admiral Hamilton, commanding the support force, sent the following message to the American cruisers under his command:

" I know that you are as sorry as I am to see this collection of brave ships abandoned in this way on the difficult route to their port."

All witnesses without exception expressed the same feeling. The Commander of *H.M.S. Keppel,* the Captain D destroyer, sent a message to the merchant ships: " Sorry to leave you like this. Good luck. Looks like a bloody business."

The Allies only released from their archives what they wished to be known. To my knowledge, the movements of

British and American warships immediately after the dispersal of the PQ 17 have never been published. It is probable that the ex-support and cover forces sailed to prevent the *Tirpitz* squadron from entering the Atlantic. Nevertheless, the Admiralty sent less and less reassuring telegrams to the escorts which were still in the dispersal zone of the convoy.

On the evening of 5th July: " Most likely time of enemy surface attack now tonight of 5th-6th, or early tomorrow morning, 6th July. Enemy may strike 065°, in direction from North Cape."

The 6th July at the same hour: "Attack by enemy surface forces is probable in the next few hours. Your primary duty is to avoid destruction to enable you to return to the scene of the attack to pick up survivors after enemy have retired."

(Here is meant, of course, the survivors of the scattered PQ 17 which the enemy surface forces were to have destroyed.)

A small group of these escort vessels without a convoy sailed under the leadership of flakship *Pozarica,* a mixed cargo converted, commanded by Captain Lawford, R.N. On the receipt of the above signal, this officer, who was the senior commander present, proposed to set a course for Novaya Zemlya instead of entering the wolf's jaws by trying to make for Archangel direct. The other captains agreed on this destination. The ships were brought together and the conference took place over the loud hailers, each captain speaking into his microphone. The sailors massed on the decks listened in deathly silence. Captain Lawford went on to speak of their conduct in the face of the enemy.

" If we are chased by destroyers we shall of course engage them. By manoeuvring we shall have a chance. If we come within range of the German battleships' guns I am sure you will agree with me that we should set our course for them and continue to fire as long as we can. But, naturally, if that happens, we can say goodbye to each other."

The witness who reports this episode insists that at that moment the sailors on all the ships burst out laughing. It was rather nervous laughter.

" I think," Captain Lawford went on, " that the men who are not on this watch would do well to get some sleep. I hope that each of you will come to terms with his conscience and place himself in the hands of his Maker. That is what I intend to do. But I also intend to lead you all to port with the help of God."

And the little fleet went resolutely on its way but expecting at any minute to see the outlines of the German mastodons loom on the horizon. But not a single German warship came in sight.

On the contrary, the wireless operators of the escorts heard successive S.O.S.s from vessels torpedoed or hit by bombs.

This is what happened on the German side.

At the moment the Admiralty ordered PQ 17 to scatter, the much-feared surface forces were at their moorings in Altenfjord, having arrived from Trondhjem. The *Tirpitz,* the *Admiral Scheer,* the *Admiral Hipper* and six destroyers left Altenfjord on the 5th July under the tactical command of Admiral Carls. But the German High Command, deceived by the reports of airmen who had indicated at least two aircraft carriers and several battleships, was little inclined to expose its last 35,000-ton battleship (the *Bismarck* had been sunk on the 27th May, 1941) and gave orders in which caution far outweighed the aggressive spirit. The *Tirpitz* squadron, hardly leaving the Norwegian coast, went for a voyage of inspection as far as twenty-five miles N.E. of Cape North. Then it put about and returned to Altenfjord, having neither met nor seen any enemy ships.

In fact, on both sides the aggressive intentions of the adversary had been over-estimated.

The part of the Arctic Ocean which the dispersed merchant ships of PQ 17 now had to cross in order to reach some Russian port (Admiralty orders left them their choice) is called the Barents Sea, after the Dutch navigator Willem Barents, the discoverer of Novaya Zemlya. The Dutchmen put to sea with a single ship in 1595. Novaya Zemlya was reached after a difficult passage: "The ice came upon us so swiftly that our hair stood up on our heads," one can read in Laharpe's account. The ship was caught in the ice-pack, lifted up and in imminent danger of breaking-up. They had to build a hut on the ice and to winter in complete darkness with provisions and means of lighting and heating which the store room and the hold of a 16th-century vessel could provide.

In the spring, unable to liberate their ship, the explorers decided to leave in a canoe and a shallop. Barents, who was a sick man, used all his strength to write his account of the expedition. This memorial was placed in a box and hung from the fireplace in the hut. It was found in perfect condition by a Norwegian captain in 1871. The hut still contained a clock, Barents' flute and sundry other objects.

The expedition left Novaya Zemlya on its return voyage on the 14th June, 1596. Barents died on the 20th. On several occasions his companions had to carry their boats over the icefields. They experienced storms, suffered from scurvy and were constantly losing their way. At last they reached the Kola Inlet at the mouth of the Murmansk and were picked up by a Dutch vessel, which took them back to their own country.

Obviously, very few of the sailors in PQ 17 had read the account of the journey of Barents and his companions. If some of them read it later they would certainly have recognised many of the aspects of their own adventure. With this difference—that in the time of Barents there were no such things as submarines or the Luftwaffe.

The *Washington* was one of the vessels which had replied stoutly to the air attack of 4th July. Her gunners had probably shot down an aircraft. She had not been hit by a bomb but near misses had bent her hull and she was shipping water.

After the convoy had been ordered to scatter, the Captain began by setting course N.N.E. like most of his colleagues. All of them wished to get as far north as possible, away from the enemy coast. The convoy advanced slowly, less in obedience to Admiralty orders than on account of the navigating conditions in a sea encumbered with ice. A general direction was followed and obstacles were avoided. In this way, the merchant ships gradually lost sight of each other.

The *Washington* sailed for a while on an empty or almost empty expanse of sea and reached the edge of an icefield. She had to skirt this obstacle. Each time an opening appeared, the Captain looked up at the Lieutenant posted in the crow's nest.

The Lieutenant then told him if it were the opening of a channel or only a crack. Sometimes he hesitated and the Captain grew impatient. He had plenty of reason to be ill-tempered and the same applied to everyone on board. Fortunately, his Lieutenant had good eyesight and the Captain was not given bad information. Not once did he engage his ship except in the more or less sinuous channels without eventually coming out in an expanse of sea. The aircraft did not appear.

About 04.00 on 15th July, the *Washington,* which had since then kept roughly on a N.N.E. course, found herself faced by a rather tall, apparently insurmountable barrier of brilliant white ice. It was the ice-pack.

The Captain had no intention of trying to reach the North Pole. But he would have preferred to have continued to the north-east before turning south to Archangel in order to expose his ship for as short a time as possible to air and U-boat attack. (He knew nothing about the messages concerning the enemy surface forces. The merchant seamen of PQ 17 had plenty of time to discuss the reasons for the withdrawal of their escort. For the moment their comments spoke volumes.) Nothing remained except to make his way along the ice-pack in a south-easterly direction.

On the morning of 5th July, the *Washington* met two British vessels (probably the *Navarino* and the *Earlston*) which had also reached the ice-pack and were skirting it. The little group sailed in company.

About 11.00 the helmsman of the *Washington* brought to the Captain on the bridge two S.O.S. messages received at a few minutes' interval. They were from the *Carlton* and *John Witherspoon,* both of which had been torpedoed by U-boats. On consulting his chart, the Captain saw that these torpedoings had taken place about fifty miles ahead of his present ship's position. He could not put about or wait until the German submarines had disappeared from the Barents Sea. The water was rising in the bottom of the *Washington* in spite of constant pumping. Moreover, he eventually had to make up his mind to cross the really dangerous waters. There was nothing to do except to press on in the direction of the danger. The men on watch were given orders to look out more carefully than ever to starboard. To port there was only the ice-pack.

While scrutinising the surface of the sea, the Captain thought of the cargo in his holds. It consisted of 350 tons of T.N.T., in perfectly watertight cases. The delicate point was this: the explosives had been loaded to starboard, in other words, on the bow from which the torpedoes would now come. A radical solution would have been to bring up the cases from the hold and throw them in the sea. But the Captain of the *Washington* still considered it his duty to try and reach a Russian port with a full cargo. He gave orders to transfer the cases of T.N.T. from starboard to port. In this way the first torpedo might not touch them off.

Between 12.00 and 14.00, other distress messages from ships of PQ 17 were intercepted.

The first assailant arrived at 15.00. It was not a submarine but a Junkers 88. The ack-ack from the three vessels opened fire as soon as it came out of the clouds. The pilot skimmed over the ships at mast height, raking them with machine-guns, then circled and ran in to drop his bombs. The gunners of the *Washington* were convinced they were going to shoot him down, but he was not even damaged. Nor were the ships damaged and there were no wounded on board the *Washington*. But the men realised that their little group had been spotted.

At 15.40, a drone was heard above the clouds; it grew louder at every second. The men listened with their hearts in their mouths. Nine Junkers came out of the clouds. The guns began to fire.

The tragedy was extremely violent and rapid. The aircraft dived in succession on the ships and the bombs rained down. In a few minutes, the three cargoes were hit and began to sink. Boats could be seen being lowered while the geysers dotted the water. By the time the aircraft disappeared, one of the vessels had already sunk. Half an hour later, all that could be seen on the sea were six lifeboats slowly making their way along the ice pack. Silence had been restored to the polar seas. The crew of the *Washington,* forty-six men all safe and sound, had got into the two boats.

Despite the speed of the shipwreck, the wireless operators had had time to send out their S.O.S. But the men in the boats were convinced that the only effect of these messages was to let the Germans know the positive result of the attack. This part of the Barents Sea was a death trap in which only the unfortunate PQ and QP convoys ventured. On the supposition that other dispersed vessels of PQ 17 were in these waters, it would be criminal to increase their chances of being attacked by directing them towards the locality of a shipwreck. All of them must be trying to force the passage as quickly as possible on a course for the Russian shore, each man for himself and God for them all.

The boats began by skirting the uninterrupted ice-pack. Then this ice seemed to be breaking up. Channels opened and to the east beyond the fields of ice they could see expanses of sea dotted with ice-blocks. Now in an easterly direction lay a shore which was not of ice but of land. Novaya Zemlya. The boats contained blankets, chocolates, pemmican, powdered milk, sugar, biscuits, dried fruit and watertight kegs of fresh water. The men began to row eastwards, making their way round the icefields. The officers reckoned that Novaya Zemlya must be a little less than 300 miles away. They were right. The sailors thought that they could cover this distance in five days' rowing. They were wrong.

At the end of the 5th July—how can one describe it as a day when it lasted for twenty-four hours?—a sailor, pointing to the west, cried: "A funnel!" The men at the oars took a breather.

The smoke increased and a vessel appeared on the horizon. The men in the boats discussed eagerly. The officers, who had kept their glasses and were looking at the new arrival, recognised it as a cargo vessel. The ship, which had heard their S.O.S., had gone off its course to pick up the shipwrecked men. It was the American cargo ship *Olopana*.

Its silhouette grew larger as it made its way round the icefields. Already the crews of the two ships sunk at the same time as the *Washington* were rowing towards it.

The two boats containing the *Washington's* crew did not move. The sailors had begun to row in that direction and then stopped. What had happened? Merely this, the shipwrecked men from the *Washington* did not wish to be picked up. They refused to go aboard the *Olopana*.

These men could still feel the deck of their ship vibrating and being raised in the air by the explosion, listing and plunging beneath their feet. They thought that it would have been madness to re-embark now in a ship which, according to them, would suffer the same fate. In their lifeboats they were comparatively secure. No plane would bother to drop bombs on them and no U-boats would torpedo them. But to board another cargo vessel was to expose themselves for certain to bombs and torpedoes. It was far better to reach the shores of Novaya Zemlya. Once they were there, the men thought, they could wait a few days until the Germans considered that their attacks on the PQ 17 were over. Then they would make their way close inshore to the south. It would be very odd if they did not meet some Russian boat. It would pick up the shipwrecked men and take them to Archangel. The dangerous area to cross would then be shorter. The sailors of the *Washington* were fully aware that something unforeseen could happen in their programme, but everything appeared preferable to going aboard the *Olopana*. They had discussed the matter while the ship was approaching and had all been in agreement. A great majority of them at least must have been of this opinion. There does not seem to have been any opposition, either on the part of the crew or, which is more important, on the part of the Captain and his officers. There is no evidence to show that the refusal to embark in the *Olopana* was the result of a mutiny.

Although this fact is not mentioned either, one can imagine that the Captain and crew of the *Olopana* were surprised to hear the refusal of the *Washington's* crew to be picked up. It is not unjustifiable to think that these men, who had replied to the S.O.S. at great risk, reproached their brothers in the *Washington* of being "ungrateful bastards." But the latter persisted in their refusal. No one asked to leave the boats. The survivors of the other two ships climbed aboard the rescuing cargo boat, which put about and sailed off. The crew of the *Washington* began to row eastwards without waiting for it to disappear to the east.

The most distressing spectacle for the shipwrecked man is obviously the vast empty expanse of sea. This huge void weighs on the spirit more than the sight of some terrifying object. These survivors, who were on a sea dotted with ice blocks, did not—at least at the outset—feel this terrible sensation of isolation. The ice broke the monotony and the eyes had something upon which to fix themselves. Land, they thought, could not be so far away and would soon appear. It would be one of those contours on the horizon or that one over there which they could already make out. But as the boat advanced, rounding and passing the ice blocks, the illusion diminished and disappeared. They found themselves as bewildered as a traveller in the desert deceived by the mirages.

The crew of the *Washington* rowed east, taking turns at the oars. They advanced through an icy sunlit seascape with bright, almost unreal, colours that reminded them of the crude images in technicolour films. At midday, the sky was cobalt blue ; sparkling bluish ice floated on a royal blue sea. These colours softened towards evening and the ice was tinged rose pink. Then the intense light returned and a new endless day began.

The 6th and 7th of July passed in this way. A dreary silence had fallen on the boat. The men at the oars shed their oilskins but put them on again and wrapped themselves in blankets as soon as they stopped rowing, for fear of catching cold. They all ate copiously to revive their strength and to protect themselves against the cold. They also drank a great deal, for these concentrated products made them thirsty.

On the morning of the 8th, the light diminished in intensity and the sky became white. The sun disappeared, and the horizon narrowed as the cloudy ceiling formed to the south-east. The light faded, as though a storm were approaching, and a breeze sprang up.

Snow began to fall. Three minutes later, between the sky and the sea, there was nothing but a mass of whirling snowflakes. At last the sky disappeared and all that remained was the uninterrupted fall of snow and the raising of a myriad moaning voices—the voices of the wind rushing against the riven ice.

In the boats the men huddled close together with their backs to the wind and heads lowered like huskies in a storm. This inertia lasted some minutes. The first spray that broke over the boats reminded them that they could not remain passive in the teeth of the snowstorm like sleigh dogs, for they were not on firm land or the ice-pack but in a small craft which was being more and more buffeted. The boats were stout metal launches with watertight bulkheads, unsinkable ; but as soon as they were allowed to drift they rapidly filled with icy water or risked capsizing. They could still sink if they hit against the ice floes. The men understood this and began to row, breasting the sea. Reliefs were frequent, for rowing in these conditions was very exhausting. The boats had lost sight of each other for the visibility was reduced to a few yards. The hubbub of the wind was very impressive, even to sailors, because of the varying tones caused by the displacement of the ice. Voices seemed to rise and fall, to call to each other and reply before roaring in chorus. Growls like dull cannon-fire were made by the ice blocks crashing together. Jagged blocks appeared all round them, for the relative speed of all these floating bodies of different sizes produced a chaotic movement. The officers shouted orders. The rowers bent to their oars without always being able to avoid the shocks. Oars broke like match sticks. Fortunately, the boats themselves were really solid. They must also have been very lucky that neither of them was crushed. The men, half blinded by the snow, almost unconscious from exhaustion in this polar wind, had lost all sense of time.

At last the snowstorm grew less intense and a few minutes later ceased as quickly as it had begun. After another half an hour the blue sky reappeared and the sun broke through. The snowstorm had lasted six hours.

The boats were about a mile apart. They joined up again. The two crews were complete, without even an

injured man. The sea calmed down and they could bale
the water from the boats and have a meal.

The tri-coloured seascape was exactly the same as it had
been six hours before. It was impossible to know how many
miles they had drifted. Their only solution was to go on
rowing towards that long curved barrier called Novaya
Zemlya, somewhere to the east. Press on!

Nothing is more distressing than to realise the first
signs of a repeated disaster. They had struggled, had con-
jured the danger, and now the same danger lay just ahead
and had to be faced with diminished strength. On the
morning of the 9th July, when the *Washington* survivors
saw the sky cloud over and darken as it had done the
previous evening, and the breeze spring up, they rebelled.
They swore and blasphemed ; some of them refused to
row any more and talked of flinging themselves overboard.
They all felt that they were victims of an intolerable piece
of injustice. They maintained that they certainly could
not suffer the ordeal of another snowstorm. It was impossible. The storm broke on them while they were still
cursing, and with cries and groans of anger they started to
row again. But at last they fell silent, for now they were
only men struggling once more and nearly at the end of
their tether.

This time, too, the snowstorm lasted exactly six hours,
and when it stopped the crews were still complete with no
injured men. But when they were nearly gunwale to gunwale, the men who were hailed fell silent. They could see
their own shipmates at close quarters and noticed that their
faces had changed since this new adventure. But the other
boat a few yards away, embossed like an old pot, now
carried a load of strangers entirely masked with salt and
ice and staring from deep-shadowed eyes. The men really
could not recognise each other from one boat to the other,
not even their own mates. It took them some time, when
at last they began to shout, to identify the voices belonging

to these faces, or rather these bearded masks covered with frost and grime.

The 9th July came to a close and they embarked upon the 10th. In this technicolour seascape both boats now rowed in sombre silence. They looked upon these sparkling blue ice blocks with utter disgust. They appeared to them as inhuman monsters, almost supernatural beings, before whom they were defenceless, completely ignored, as though they were already dead, rowing obstinately and absurdly in a watery beyond which there would never be a landfall. More than one must have thought of the *Olopana* and their refusal, but by intuitive prudence the name was never once mentioned. This spark would probably have touched off a terrible explosion of despair. The crew of the *Washington* could not know, of course, that the *Olopana* had gone down on the 6th, sunk by the torpedo of a U-boat.

On the 10th July, a bird appeared in the sky. Was it really a bird? While the men raised their owlish masks to the cobalt blue, others cried: " Land ahoy! " waving wildly. They could all see it and there could be no mistake. That continuous barrier high on the horizon could only be land. The men shouted for joy. They started to row with all their might. Everyone was in a high state of nervous tension. Some said that they would land within two or three hours, but the officers, having judged the distance, decided that they had another ten hours' rowing, if not more, and that it was better to row steadily. The men had a big meal to recover their strength and also because their emotion had made them very hungry.

Novaya Zemlya is a prolongation of the Ural Chain, a mole hardly separated from the Russian continent, advancing into the Arctic Ocean as far as latitude 77°. This 500-mile long promontory, covering an area of 45,000 square miles, is split into two distinct islands at the seventy-third parallel by a remarkable channel known as Matotchkin Shar. It is a transversal fjord, open at both ends, more than sixty miles long and at the most a mile and a half wide, very narrow in places and constantly dominated by hills 3,000 feet high. These hills have Alpine type glaciers and the most spectacular ravines. In the summer their slopes are covered with green fields of dryas alternating with willows and dwarf birches.

Animal life is almost non-existent in Novaya Zemlya, except in the plains of the southern island, where a few lemmings, wild reindeer, foxes, wolves and bears are to be found. In the fjords and off the shores the waters teem with salmon, cod and herring, seals and whales. Seabirds nest at the top of the cliffs. Since the seventeenth century, on the western beaches, pieces of driftwood have been found from ships which had been wrecked in the Barents Sea.

In Navigation Instructions one can read: "A colony of some dozen Russians and Samoyeds live on the shore of the southern island at the entrance to Matotchkin Shar.

The crew of the *Washington* landed on the 12th July on the north-west coast of Novaya Zemlya. They did not know their exact whereabouts.

The two boats beached and the men leaped ashore.

Just beyond the beach were marvellously green hills and behind them taller snow-capped mountains. The peaks were clearly outlined against the bright blue sky. But the survivors were looking at the green slopes of the hills. They saw that they were covered with short grass, and this colour touched their hearts and nearly moved them to tears.

They walked towards these hills. They had been so wretched during their week's crossing in an icy hostile sea that all of them now felt they were making for a hospitable land where man should be able to dwell. On the pebbles, wild geese stared at them, hardly bothering to fly off.

They climbed the first slope and stopped. Ahead of them stretched a motionless undulating landscape of huge frozen waves which were snowy, icy mountains, gleaming in the sun. This petrified storm stretched to the horizon and there was no sign of life. They walked back to the beach in silence.

It was bitterly cold in spite of the sun. The night before, the provisions in the boats had been exhausted. Obviously, the only resources of this land were the birds which peopled the shore. They managed to capture eight wild geese which they killed. The ensign shot a gull. The sound of the shot broke the great silence and echoed through the hills. The birds and geese rose in flocks. From that moment all of them kept their distance. Everyone returned to the boats and cooked a soup.

The sailors did not know exactly at what latitude they had landed but they knew that they now had to head south. Revived, they re-embarked and began to row along the coast. They rowed for the second part of 12th July, twenty-four hours of the 13th and the whole morning of the 14th without eating. The shore was quite deserted. On several occasions they shot at gulls but did not manage to kill one. At the first shot all the birds flew off rapidly. The men were suffering from weariness, hunger and cold. A few of them noticed that their legs were swollen and that they could no longer feel their feet.

The 14th July brought a change. About the middle of the day, they met four lifeboats full of survivors from the Dutch cargo vessel *Paulus Potter,* one of the PW ships which had also been sunk after the convoy had scattered. This meeting comforted everyone. The survivors of the *Paulus Potter* were as destitute as those of the *Washington,* but now everyone thought that things would be better. There were more of them and they would get out of it. Excitedly they told each other of their adventures, made plans without always understanding each other, but that did not matter. Obviously, the first thing was to get some food. The men of the *Paulus Potter* said that they had seen some wild duck not far away and everyone went ashore. They were right. A well-organised attack procured 100 birds, about one per man. The morale rose. It would have risen even higher had not a third of the men discovered that their feet were definitely frost-bitten. They could hardly walk.

After eating the duck, the fleet of six boats rowed south along the coast. Several of the officers kept a kind of log book of the expedition. In one of them we can read: " 15th July. Rowed in the direction of the Russian mainland." The nearest point of the Russian mainland was 350 miles away!

But the 15th brought a new meeting which was of great interest. Rounding a small cape the shipwrecked men saw a few hundred yards ahead a motionless ship near the shore. To them it looked enormous. It was the American cargo vessel *Winston Salem,* another member of PQ 17. She had floundered on a sandbank.

Incapable of refloating without assistance, the *Winston Salem* was still in good condition with a lighted boiler, the galley and refrigerator well stocked. For the shipwrecked men this meant shelter, warmth, food and rest. Later they all spoke of this beached cargo vessel as of a paradise, and it is impossible to read the accounts of these simple sea-faring men without being moved. Their joy makes one understand what they had endured for eleven days.

The men with frostbite received attention. The crews of the *Washington* and the *Paulus Potter* remained two days aboard this ship. They would willingly have remained longer. They were a colony of Robinson Crusoes, enjoying every comfort, forgotten by the warring outside world.

The outside world manifested itself on the third day in the form of a ship which appeared on the horizon to the south and was later identified as a Soviet whaler. The new arrival anchored not far from the *Winston Salem* without beaching. A boat was sent ashore. In it were two Russians with Mongol faces, dressed in bearskins and fur caps. They came aboard and let it be understood that other ships, English or American, were not far away. They offered to transport any who wished towards these ships. The survivors could not abuse much longer the hospitality of the

Winston Salem, whose provisions were getting low, so with regret they left their haven and went aboard the whaler, promising the Captain of the American vessel that they would send him help. The beached vessel was refloated a little later.

The whaler coasted southwards. This form of navigation was certainly less exhausting than rowing in the boats. But the hours passed and the survivors were surprised not to see the Allied ships which had been reported. They questioned the Russians who replied in an incomprehensible tongue. The Dutch and American officers identified the entrance to the famous Matotchkin Shar but the whaler passed without stopping. There was a lighthouse and two wooden huts. A little farther off a few more huts, also of wood. They could distinguish a dozen men, two women, a few children and dogs around these huts. They all stood side by side on the shore, motionless, watching the ship pass without replying to the greetings of the Allied sailors. Who were these people? What were they doing there? And what a miserable life they must lead. Were they deportees? The survivors began to feel uneasy. They wondered if the Allied ships really existed somewhere and how far these Mongol fishermen whom it was impossible to understand were going to lead them.

At last, after about sixteen hours' sailing, a shape which the men recognised appeared at the end of a bay. It was the British merchant ship *Empire Tide,* another vessel from the convoy. The survivors left the whaler, to their relief.

They were in store for a disagreeable surprise aboard the *Empire Tide.* She had picked up other survivors and the boat was full. The arrival of these new shipwrecked men would bring their complement up to 240. Practically no provisions and a famine regime. . . . The *Empire Tide* had been chased by a U-boat as far as the entrance to the Matotchkin Shar. She had entered the fjord and remained hidden there for several days. Then she had come out and sailed as far as this bay—Moller Bay. The Captain could not make up his mind to continue without escort with all these men aboard.

The Russian whaler had now disappeared to the south and the men saw a plane circling far away out of range. It must have been one of those hawks which they knew only too well and now it was sending messages. The crew of the *Washington* began to swear. The bombers would soon appear. Why had they not remained aboard the *Winston Salem*?

Those men had already taken a few important decisions. They had decided not to wait passively for a bombing attack which would certainly wreak havoc on this over-populated floating town. Since the Captain of the *Empire Tide* could not make up his mind to set sail (this decision was comprehensible) and since he could not feed them, the *Washington* crew asked to be allowed to go ashore in the two boats, taking a few tents for shelter. The gunner ensign declared that he would remain aboard with his men, but the others insisted and the Captain of the *Empire Tide* granted their request. They got into the boat and camped ashore.

They remained there forty-eight hours, suffering from the cold and living sparsely on a few birds, but the food was no better in the ship. Contrary to the general opinion, no German bomber had appeared.

Early on 20th July the Captain of the *Empire Tide* told the campers that he had received a radio message from a British warship and that he was going to sail. They returned aboard.

A few hours later the *Empire Tide* joined the remains of PQ 17, which had been rounded up by several escort vessels. This formation, which consisted of five cargo boats, six armed sloops and British flakships, three corvettes from the Free French forces and two Russian destroyers, finally entered the port of Archangel on 25th July, three weeks after the dispersal of the convoy. The sick men were sent to the Russian hospital where the Allied naval attachés visited them. A dozen of the *Washington* ship's company had frost-bitten feet, but they had not lost a man.

From the 4th to the 15th July the Barents Sea had been transformed into a murderous arena. The pursued ships, making slow headway through the icefields, occasionally met the protection of a fog bank. Hardly had it dispersed or been crossed than they found swarms overhead which harrassed, machine-gunned and bombed them. If the victim was still afloat when the attackers left others immediately flew over from the shore to give them the *coup de grâce*.

At midnight on the 4th July (we must not forget that it was full daylight) the liberty ship *Daniel Morgan,* sailing in company with her sister ship *Samuel Chase,* saw a British flakship draw alongside. It sent the following signal: " The *Tirpitz* is on her way with other warships. I'm going to take shelter in a Novaya Zemlya bay. Advise you to do the same."

The two liberty ships met three other vessels and then the fog came down. When it rose the *Daniel Morgan* found that her four companions had disappeared and in their place discovered a sixth fugitive of the convoy, the *Fairfield City*. A minute later three Junkers 88s appeared. The *Fairfield City* was sunk in a matter of seconds. The *Daniel Morgan* put up a defence for several hours. Flights of bombers continued to arrive in threes or fives while she zig-zagged about the sea, hitting ice blocks and continuing to fire. She continued until her ammunition ran out. She was shipping water through the plates buckled by near misses. The Captain gave orders to abandon ship. The men had hardly taken to the boats than the wake of a torpedo could be seen as it sped across the sea. Their ship was rocked by an explosion and sank. At this moment they saw a submarine surface. The German crew appeared on the deck and motioned them to approach. The Commander of the U-boat said to them in English: " If you row due east you'll find land two hundred miles away."

In the meantime some of the German officers were photographing the boats.

In the tale of a war correspondent, I have read that the U-boat captain gave a box of biscuits and a keg of fresh water to the shipwrecked men while the scene was being filmed. True, the author tells us that the men were not in a boat but on a raft, conferring a piece of odious irony upon the invitation to make a trip of two hundred miles. In actual fact the survivors of the *Daniel Morgan* were in boats, and on the following day they were picked up by the Soviet tanker *Donbass* (also among the PQ 17 which eventually reached Archangel). Distortion of the truth for patriotic propaganda purposes seems in this case to be a monumental piece of futility. It is obvious that the attacking aircraft and submarines were accomplishing no humanitarian task in the Barents Sea but a ruthless task of destruction. The story of PQ 17 is dramatic enough; there was no necessity to add anything.

The *Samuel Chase,* also fleeing before the supposed enemy surface vessels, reached Novaya Zemlya, entering Matotchkin Shar where it found several other survivors of the PQ 17. One of these ships bore on the hull a name which evoked the bitterest reflections—*Ocean Freedom*. On the 7th July several escort vessels, among them the *Pozarica,* which we have already mentioned, joined the assembly. A convoy consisting of six merchant ships and ten small warships was formed ; destination Archangel.

The *Benjamin Harrison,* one of their number, disappeared the following day in the fog. The convoy was attacked from the 9th July at 22.00 to the 10th July at 05.30 without interruption except for an interval of ten minutes. The gunners, completely deafened, suffered terribly from inflamed eyes as a result of staring up into the sun. When the action finished the bravest men showed signs of complete exhaustion. Two bombers had been shot down but they had lost two ships, the *Hoozier* and the *El Capitan.*

The others arrived at Iokanka, Molotovsk and Archangel on the 11th July.

The story of the *Benjamin Harrison* which disappeared in the fog on the 7th and the ships which rejoined her is probably the most picturesque of all those in the dispersed convoy.

This vessel reached the entrance to Matochkin Shar on the 8th July when the little convoy we have recently described had already set sail. She was joined on the following day by the sloop *H.M.S. Ayrshire,* which was escorting two British ships and the Panamanian *Troubadour.*

The Captain of the *Troubadour,* George J. Salvesen, was an old hand at Arctic navigation. In actual fact his brilliant idea could have been thought out by any man of ingenuity. After inspecting the stores in his hold Salvesen went aboard the *Ayrshire* and submitted his plan to the Captain. The latter found it good and sent out the order: "Paint all the ships white."

At the same time the remains of the convoy entered Matotchkin Shar at three knots behind the *Troubadour* which, with its reinforced bows, acted as ice breaker. But time was precious and so was the paint. Since the enemy could only come from the south, only the starboard decks, hulls and superstructures were painted. The ships which had not enough paint to camouflage themselves entirely had orders to stretch sheets and table linen on the deck.

On the 10th July, these phantom ships were rejoined in Matotchkin Shar by two Russian cargo boats, a tanker and an armed sloop, all ex-PQ 17. The captains of these vessels rallied stoutly to this idea of camouflage in white and their crews were soon busy with their paint brushes.

These semi-camouflaged ships forced their way into Matotchkin Shar as far as the ice would allow. When they could not advance they anchored in line ahead beneath the mountains of Novaya Zemlya. A German aircraft flying over these mountains failed to spot them. They remained there for two weeks. When they felt that the sector was calmer they left the fjord and sailed to Archangel, where their arrival on the 25th July caused a sensation. But the whole fleet had arrived safely.

The balance sheet of the PQ 17 was as follows: Total number of merchant ships sunk, twenty-two out of thirty-three.

This number does not include the rescue ship *Zaafaran* nor the British naval tanker *H.M.S. Aldersdale*, also sunk.

Of the ships sunk fifteen were American, six British and one Dutch. Seven Americans and two British arrived at their destination, as well as two Soviet merchant ships.

The cargo sunk was 123,000 out of 188,000 tons.

I have been unable to discover the loss of human life. One reads in the reports that on the 4th August, 1942, 1,300 survivors, all from the sunk ships, entered the Kola Inlet. That is to say, they had been assembled at Murmansk to await repatriation. A pleasant stay for the survivors, as one can easily imagine! The cruiser *Tuscalousa* took 240 aboard on the 23rd August; others returned home later, some of them much later, others not at all. They were killed in the bombing of Murmansk.

It was among the survivors of this convoy that the neurologists and army psychiatrists found the best part of their clientele.

A few shipwrecked men from this convoy were picked up off the Norwegian coast by a German minesweeper or armed sloop which a British submarine sank almost immediately. .Fished out of the sea once more by another German vessel, these survivors remained prisoners until the end of the war, in Bremen. Those who survived the bombing attacks of the liberators could not have been in much better shape than their comrades from Murmansk.

The German official historians found the exact nomenclature for the PQ 17: " The massacred convoy."

CHAPTER SEVEN

Iceland Interlude

MANY OF THE SAILORS IN THESE CONVOYS only knew Iceland from seeing it as they sailed along the coast or anchored in the roads—the green or white shore, according to the season, the background of mountains with the volcano Hekla, the waterfalls, toy villages and the bright-coloured roofs of Reykjavik. Nevertheless some of them went ashore for a few hours while others remained for longer periods in the military hospital or as convalescents. As a general rule none of them retained a very pleasant memory of their stay, either because it had been too short to allow them to discover the natural beauties of Iceland or because in their eyes it was in the nature of an exile. Some of them, however, judged Iceland objectively, realising that had they been there in different circumstances they would probably have liked the country.

The first impression of sailors going ashore at Reykjavik was one of pleasant surprise. The dazzling white houses with their gleaming black, red, pink or pale green roofs, the clean busy streets, the attractive shops, were a contrast after the images they had brought back from their sinister visit to Murmansk or Archangel. The newcomers, who had expected to find a semi-savage population more or less dressed in skins, admired the Icelandic girls in their bright coloured dresses and sweaters, pretty shoes and nylon stockings. This modern town of 45,000 inhabitants seemed prosperous and in actual fact it was. In the shops were to be found practically everything that could be bought in the

United States. Nearly all the goods actually came from the States or Great Britain.

The sailors naturally visited the shops to buy presents and souvenirs. They bought scarves, cushion covers, book covers with painted or embroidered Icelandic scenes, seal-skin gloves and purses, babies' sleeping bags, sheepskin coverlets and above all magnificent sweaters in unbleached wool with bright patterns like Fair Isles. These sweaters were the rage back home where sailors' and soldiers' wives wore them with pride.

The shop girls were nearly all young, smart, well-built and pretty, speaking fluent English with a slight accent. They were good and courteous tradeswomen but always refused to go out with the troops. This general refusal was the first disappointment in store for the sailor who went ashore at Reykjavik.

The men eventually frequented the American Red Cross recreation centre ; it was in Nissen huts in the middle of the town where there was plenty of space. The occupation authorities made praiseworthy efforts to find amusement for the troops. There were libraries, writing rooms, ping-pong and billiards tables, cards, chess, draughts, dominoes, a bowling green and other games. The gloomy visitors wandered like phantoms from one room to another, waiting for a film show, which changed each day, or the free bi-weekly distribution of nut fritters. The visitors could also buy coca-cola and non-alcoholic drinks for a song.

This centre also had a ballroom which was open twice a week, but there was hardly any attendance. The pretty Icelanders did not come to the dance any more than they accepted the other invitations. So the sailor on shore leave more often than not returned aboard laden with souvenirs but disillusioned.

We shall now deal with the servicemen who stayed for longer periods in Reykjavik.

On disembarkation they were taken by truck to a camp some miles from the town. This camp, also in a Nissen hut, offered all the comforts which the inexhaustible wealth of America could procure for her troops. There were living quarters, messes and dining halls, a hospital, sick wards, bath and showers, a cinema, a post and exchange office and a chapel. The men had books, magazines and wireless sets at their disposal. The walls of their bright well-heated huts were decorated with photographs of pin-up girls. In spite of this they were all comfortably bored.

The first Icelanders with whom they had contact were the children who constantly wandered round the camp. Although the adults were very reserved (they had proclaimed their independence after the invasion of Denmark, to whom the island previously belonged, and were annoyed that they had been occupied by the Allies) the children showed pro-Allied sentiments since they had their own axe to grind. Their first words were always: " Give me candy, or gum." The Anglo-Saxons could not refuse the children anything. They gave generously whatever was asked of them. The little boys said " thank you " and the little girls gave them a smile. Delicious smiles from children with fair hair and rosy cheeks. They very quickly improved the English they had learned at school. Several of them were allowed into the camp to sell magazines.

The men in the camp could go to Reykjavik in the Iceland buses or in their own trucks. The capital offered them the pleasures and disappointments we have already described. For their entertainment the military authorities often organised tourist excursions in the summer. The Army provided transport and the Red Cross, lunches—ham sandwiches, sausage, cheese, potato salad, pickles, cakes and fruit and the inevitable coca-cola. The excursions lasted all day, in other words about twenty hours. The troops were taken to see the most magnificent spectacles of nature: lakes unrivalled in their blue limpidity, set like mirrors in jade green fields, glorious leaping waterfalls, boiling geysers at the foot of icy mountains ; meadows of wild flowers trembling in the breeze. " These excursions were very much appreciated by new arrivals," said Corporal Luther M. Chovan.

The trouble taken by the occupying authorities was untiring, and it is understandable that they were ready to do all they could to raise a smile from their men. Realising that they had exhausted the pleasure of buying in the shops, they opened a huge Army store where the men found exactly the same object displayed in exactly the same way as in the Woolworths or the American five and ten cents stores. " This innovation was good for the morale," says a witness, " for there was an abundance of ice cream, popcorn, sweets, soap, razor blades, socks and cigarette cases."

Natives were used as shop assistants—a few youths and a great many girls. Although the girls with their shapely legs encased in nylon stockings worked in this Allied store and were pestered by their customers, they invariably refused to make dates with the same polite obstinacy. " One day," Corporal Chovan told me, " I asked a girl who was waiting with me at the bus stop why the population was so reserved and almost hostile towards us. She replied that there were too many of us and that soldiers always tried to flirt." Poor soldiers. " It is true," added Chovan, " that the behaviour of servicemen had not been always very gentlemanly, so the disapproval extended to the uniform. The Icelanders all seemed arrogant, proud and distant. Of course they had the right to be proud since they had possessed a democratic government for more than a thousand years." This conclusion is really rather touching.

The truth is that at the beginning of the occupation a certain number of young Iceland girls had become engaged to Allied soldiers who, as is well known, attached little importance to these war-time betrothals. For the Icelanders, on the other hand, any sentimental relationship is a serious matter. One day the fiancé left Iceland and was never heard of again. This did a grave social wrong to the girl, not to mention her more or less broken heart. The mothers, who wield enormous authority, insisted that their daughters should keep their distance. There were no exceptions.

It is interesting to note that this reserve finally modified the behaviour of the Allied servicemen towards the girls of Iceland. Men who remained for some time in the country realised the futility of casual invitations and insistence. The girls were treated by the Americans with infinitely more respect than was displayed to the women of the numerous countries they crossed or occupied. " Even the rakes became courteous and considerate." This modification of relations allowed deeper sentiments than the men had hitherto envisaged to blossom since a hundred or so marriages were performed, all of them enduring, according to official information. In actual fact there could be no basic incompatibility between these daughters of the Vikings and the Anglo-Saxons.

As a result of this, in the role of serious and accepted fiancés, a few Allied soldiers and sailors were invited into Icelandic homes and were able to discover the virtues of this small nation where illiteracy is unknown, and where bookshops flourish per head of the population better than anywhere else in the world. It is true that in winter the evenings are long!

The courtship which took place in the presence of the parents began at half past three with coffee, sandwiches and cakes. One of the young girls would play the piano or sing. After supper at about seven o'clock the young people danced—swing, waltzes or jitterbug. Then the guests said " thank you " very politely and withdrew. No meetings outside were possible. Apparently only a small number of servicemen got to know this family aspect of life in Iceland. The others continued to pay occasional visits to the ball-room in the rest centre, where there was still a dearth of girls. The most optimistic reports maintain that there were about forty at Christmas, 1943, but a *Life* reporter insisted that there were never more than half a dozen.

Those who enjoyed winter sports could practise ski-ing

or skating on Lake Jörnin in the centre of Reykjavik. The girls skated like professionals. If anyone suggested that he should partner a girl on the ice she simply replied: "No thank you."

A very few of the soldiers and sailors had occasion to get on very cordial terms with the natives. These were men who were not afraid of travelling far into the country and visiting the farms. They found houses provided with every modern convenience and decorated with taste. The peasants used the most modern methods of cultivation, exploiting with remarkable intelligence the resources of their strange country. In hothouses heated by the water from volcanic geysers they grew tomatoes, cucumbers and even bananas. The young farm girls in white blouses kept poultry in ultra-modern chicken runs and the stables were more like laboratories. On Sunday the whole family went for a ride on ponies (Iceland has a pony which can take three people on its back). The women wore trousers, sweaters and bright coloured scarves on their heads. Those who had known how to arouse the sympathy of these frank pleasant people were taken on these excursions. They visited the waterfalls, picnicked, returned home late, singing and admiring the splendours of the Aurora Borealis.

"In order to love Iceland you have to love nature," concluded Corporal Luther M. Chovan.

CHAPTER EIGHT

The Black Planes

THE DISASTROUS BALANCE SHEET OF CON-
voy PQ 17 (twenty-two ships sunk out of thirty-three) was
published first in the United States. Journalists and poli-
ticians bitterly criticised the orders given by the British
Admiralty with regard to this convoy. The emotion finally
reached Great Britain where it manifested itself more
discreetly. The Admiralty apparently remained undaunted.
It had already taken the two decisions which, in the eyes of
the Sea Lords, were correct.

The first of these decisions, which was kept a top secret,
was to strain every effort towards a certain plan which
would be mentioned when the time was ripe. The second
was this: to send no more convoys across the Arctic Ocean
until the days drew in. The uninterrupted daylight gave
too great an advantage to the Luftwaffe based in Norway,
and no adequate protection could be given. Therefore the
convoys were suspended and the Admiralty said: "Wait
and see." When circumstances were more favourable they
would see if the programme could be continued and at
what rhythm.

This decision was reported to the Soviet High Command,
which protested energetically. The U.S.S.R. was hard
pressed by the German offensive and her troops had more
need than ever of war material and munitions.

On reading the notes which their eastern ally sent on
this subject, the British and Americans were amazed to
find that the Russians did not believe that the losses in the
convoys were as high as stated. This was not actually ex-

pressed, but the text and the tone of these Soviet notes leaves no doubt as to their convictions. The Russians, having seen the arrival in their ports of eleven cargoes from PQ 17, among them two Soviet vessels which had left Scotland with the convoy, refused to admit that twenty-two merchant ships were sunk. It will be said that they might have found out for themselves by questioning the captains of their two ships, who had seen the whole convoy with their own eyes. Probably they preferred not to question them, or simply not to believe them. It is also possible that the captains preferred not to run into trouble by stubbornly sticking to the truth. In any case, the Soviet authorities replied to the British notes, ostentatiously avoiding replying to the terms of these notes which stressed the appalling losses of the convoys. They still did not believe or did not wish to believe. Marshal Stalin wrote directly to Winston Churchill, complaining that the army and the Soviet population were bearing the entire brunt of the war and that the provision of arms and ammunition could in no circumstances be interrupted. The whole outcome of the war, he insisted, depended on this.

The British Prime Minister, having for several years been First Lord of the Admiralty, will have known what was possible and what was impossible. The decision not to dispatch any convoys at least until September was maintained. Nevertheless, in order not to leave the Marshal without the slightest satisfaction, the Admiralty announced that it would send a special task force of transports consisting of warships. For this mission three American units were detailed—the 10,000-ton heavy cruiser *Tuscalousa* and the destroyers *Emmons* and *Rodman*.

On the 12th August the *Tuscalousa* took on at Greenock three hundred tons of ammunition, explosives, radar parts, medical supplies, dehydrated foods, and thirty-six torpedoes. Each destroyer carried twenty tons of aircraft parts and nineteen tons of mixed cargo. Seven British naval officers, three R.A.F. officers and 160 other passengers sailed with the three ships. This task force left Greenock on the 13th August after a stay of several days at Scapa Flow. (The Admiralty wished to gain time.) It arrived on the 19th at Seydisfjordhur in Iceland, and put to sea again the same day. It crossed the Arctic Ocean at full speed, arriving at Murmansk on the 23rd. No one wished to stay at Murmansk longer than was absolutely necessary. The warships unloaded and set sail the following day, having taken on 240 survivors of PQ 17 out of the 1,300 who were still there, and 300 other passengers, including four Russian diplomats. The return voyage was also made at full speed without incident apart from meeting a German minelayer, which was sunk by gunfire.

During the whole of this time Stalin and his High Command continued to sue for help. The cargoes brought by the *Tuscalousa* task force were ridiculously inadequate. Since there was no question of continuing to use warships as transports, the Admiralty decided to form another convoy, the PQ 18, which set sail from Loch Ewe on the 2nd September, 1942.

It would perhaps be redundant to relate even briefly the tragic journey of PQ 18. The reader might grow weary and find it monotonous. The same tragedy, when repeated or even described with variety, always has this effect on the spectator. And yet in this appalling repetition lies the real tragedy, for the spectators to consent for a moment to put themselves in the place of those who live it, with the risk of meeting their death each time. The combatants never find their battle monotonus even if it resembles the preceding one in every detail.

The voyage of PQ 18, however, bore little resemblance to that of PQ 17. The convoy was not dispersed and there were only thirteen ships sunk out of thirty-three. But if the PQ 17 held the record for ships sunk the PQ 18 was the convoy which was subjected to the most violent air attacks in the course of its journey.

It set sail from Scotland on the 2nd September just before the arrival of the survivors of PQ 17 in Great Britain. But although the détails were lacking, the news of " the massacred convoy " were already known in naval circles. The crews of the merchant vessels and of the warships knew that they were about to sail in waters which had been rendered almost impassable by aircraft and submarines, not to mention the threat of the appearance of big German surface units. The sight of the powerful escort (the 17,000-ton aircraft carrier *H.M.S. Avenger,* carrying fifteen planes ; the light 5,450-ton anti-aircraft cruiser *H.M.S. Scylla* ; sixteen destroyers, two submarines, and several small craft) was not enough to reassure the merchant seamen. They thought of the unpleasant precedent and nothing assured them that they would not be left by their protectors in the middle of the danger zone. A certain number of them had already been shipwrecked in convoy PQ 16, partially destroyed by enemy action, or on their return journey with QP 13, several of whose ships were blown up in a minefield. A few of them had been shipwrecked both on the outwards and homeward journey.

Nothing happened between Loch Ewe and Iceland, nor during the first few days after leaving Reykjavik. The first enemy spotter aircraft appeared on the 12th September. It came out of the clouds far to the south of the convoy and flew off immediately before the *Avenger* had time to head into the wind and launch her Hurricanes. The wireless operators heard its messages.

The bombers would not arrive immediately, for their range was less than that of the recco plane ; but the convoy would soon be entering their operational zone. It had been spotted and its route was known. Warships which are to engage the enemy can often outwit him by manoeuvring and taking unexpected routes. A convoy transporting material from one port to another, skirting the ice-pack, cannot act in this way. It advances like a tram on rails.

The first attack took place in the early morning of 13th September. Two merchant ships were sunk by U-boats. The latter, notified by the spotter, had taken up their position exactly in their path. After firing their " tin fish " they had only to send a message in turn, saying that the tramway convoy was advancing at the exact speed predicted. This progress was followed eagerly in Berlin because of the strategic importance taken on by the naval theatre of war in the Arctic Ocean. On a map like the one hanging on the wall in the subterranean hall of Liverpool, officers and officials of the *Kriegsmarine* also stuck in their little flags. The game had started.

None of the crews of PQ 18 had been surprised by the nature of this first attack which, one might almost say, was classic: one of the escort destroyers, breaking off with much blowing of whistles, the wakes of torpedoes speeding over the sea, ships weaving in apparent confusion and finally two waterspouts and explosions from the ships hit ; some way off, destroyers and corvettes dropping depth charges ; boats leaving the sinking ships . . .

The aircraft attacked the convoy the same afternoon as soon as it was within range of the Norwegian air bases. At that moment it was a little to the west of Spitzbergen. First to appear were about a dozen bombers flying at altitude. They had probably received orders to locate the convoy before bombing it, to attract the attention of the *Avenger's* fighters and in this way to leave the field free for more formidable assailants which were to follow.

But the carrier's aircraft did not take off, for the very good reason that they were already airborne. According to reports they were on a reconnaissance flight. The tactics of aircraft carriers was a tricky matter and would not be perfected until much later. The captains of these vessels were always liable to commit one or two of the following errors: to launch the planes too soon, which resulted in a risk of not intercepting the enemy or being there at the moment of attack, or to launch them too late, in which case the carrier risked being attacked before it was in position or during its manoeuvre. On the occasion of this first air attack of 13th September, the *Avenger's* Hurricanes were airborne. Fortunately, the enemy bombed from too great a height and no ship was hit. But the *Avenger's* planes had not yet returned before the more formidable enemy appeared half an hour later. This was more serious.

They were torpedo-carrying planes—thirty to forty Junkers 88s and a similar number of Heinkel 115s. Flying low in three sections, they attacked with great resolution as though the ack-ack from the ships did not exist. And yet, according to eyewitnesses, the volume of fire was impressive and, some say, terrifying. They flew fifty feet above the waves and pressed home the attack on the convoy " with suicidal courage." Among them were planes of a strange colour which the sailors on the Russian run had never seen before—black with orange or green painted wings. These were squadrons from the Mediterranean, piloted by the cream of the Luftwaffe. The German High Command had sent for them specially to attack the convoys. They did not launch their torpedoes until they had only just room enough to pull out before crashing into the target. They rose slowly like magpies, passed a few feet above the masts, riddled with shells. The example of these gamblers with death aroused the fanaticism of all the other attackers. Some of them caught fire, fell into the sea, but none of them failed to press home his attack. The Commodore of the convoy gave his orders by siren blasts to carry out a 45° change of course, but the din was so terrific that many of the vessels did not even hear it. In actual fact they were all weaving like tracked beasts. The warships fired on the planes until the moment when they would have hit their own ships. The trajectories of their shells crossing the fire of the ship singled out as target, formed a net of fire over the sea. In spite of this, the Luftwaffe pressed home its attack. There were now more than 100 planes in the air round the convoy. Above the deafening din of the ack-ack could be heard the explosions of ships hit by torpedoes. In every ship the crew was certain that it was quite impossible that their own vessel could come unscathed through this inferno.

They had not all been right. Not all, but a great number. When the planes of the *Avenger* returned, six of the convoy had been sent to the bottom and fifteen enemy planes had been shot down.

The following morning at three o'clock, another U-boat torpedoed and sank a tanker. It immediately sent a message to say that the tramway convoy was continuing on the same course. The torpedo-bombers arrived at 13.00 in the same strength as on the previous day. This time the *Avenger's* aircraft were in readiness. The carrier manoeuvred and they took off. The combat was now different to that of the previous day. As far as one can judge from eyewitness accounts, it must have resembled on a reduced scale the gigantic air-sea battles in the Pacific. A reduction in numbers but not in intensity. It must be considered almost a miracle that none of the Hurricanes were shot down by the ack-ack from the ships. " The Jerry planes passed so close that it was impossible to miss them with a machine-gun." I have not been able to trace the number of Junkers and Heinkels shot down, and perhaps the figures were never given. The record for the day was held by an American merchant ship, the *Nathaniel Green,* which accounted for five. " Congratulations to your gunners," signalled the Commodore, " you are top of the class." At one moment a terrible explosion shook the *Nathaniel Green.* As they had spotted four tracks, everyone aboard thought that the ship had been torpedoed ; the Captain stopped his engines and gave the order to abandon ship. At this moment, the chief engineer arrived on deck and cried: " Everything's okay below." The order was belayed and the crew returned to action stations. Several of the gun's crew having been seriously wounded, one of the escort destroyers came along-side to take them off. A little later, when the ship had rejoined the convoy, the Captain learned that his ship had been blasted by the explosion of the *Mary Luckenbach,* 150 yards away. Everything had been destroyed on deck, doors torn out, the sick bay put out of action and the compasses out of service. But the *Nathaniel Green* rejoined the convoy and sailed on. The Captain, George A. Vickers, was congratulated on his *sang-froid.* Reserve Ensign Billings, the gunnery officer, declared: "Although paralysed with fright, all my men obeyed me implicitly. No one could be more proud of his men than I am." Two or three more ships were sunk during this attack.

The following morning, 15th September, the convoy was attacked by a pack of U-boats. The escorting destroyers attacked with depth charges but without result. The Luftwaffe arrived in the afternoon according to routine. Fortunately, they were only high altitude bombers. The Hurricanes from the *Avenger* engaged them and brought down several. No ship was hurt.

Other U-boats attacked without result on the following morning. To the general surprise there were no aircraft. That evening, *H.M.S. Avenger, H.M.S. Scylla* and most of the escort left to protect the home-bound convoy QP 14. The crews grew nervous. The enemy airfields were now less than 150 miles away.

They were attacked once more on the 18th as they entered the White Sea by high altitude and torpedo bombers and on the next two days by heavy bombers off Archangel. One ship was sunk by the torpedo-carrying aircraft.

" For several days we only slept two hours out of the twenty-four," Ensign Miller, gunnery officer of the merchant ship *St. Olaf,* wrote in his diary. " The men fed at their action stations. There were nineteen hours of daylight, during which no one left his post. Our life-saving suits were a torture to our exhausted bodies, but we could not take them off for the water was very cold, and if the

ship had to be abandoned quickly we should never have
had time to put them on."

Convoy PQ 18 reached Molotovsk at last on the 21st
September. As we have already said, thirteen of its ships
had been sunk.

The PQ 18's escort had left to take charge of QP 14 on
the 13th September. This convoy was not subjected to a
single air attack throughout its crossing, but it met submarines. The first of these U-boats was sunk on the 14th
by the British destroyer *H.M.S. Onslow;* on the 16th the
destroyer *H.M.S. Impulsive* sank a second. But before these
victims disappeared they had signalled the position and
route of the convoy to Admiral Schniewind's headquarters
at Narvik. These details were transmitted to Admiral
Doenitz at Lorient, the centre for all U-boat communications.

Other U-boats followed the QP 14 at extreme distance
of visibility, and as soon as a pack had collected, " *rudel-
taktik* " was put into operation. Between the 20th and
22nd of September, the U-boats attacked the convoy twenty
times, penetrating it at night and slipping away by day
without losing contact. The pack was constantly increased
by new arrivals. The following ships were sunk: the British
destroyer *H.M.S. Somali,* a minesweeper, a tanker and three
merchant ships. Two of the latter, the Americans *Belling-
ham* and *Silver Sword,* were survivors of PQ 17, finally
bringing the record of the massacred convoy up to twenty-
four merchant ships sunk out of thirty-three (plus a rescue
launch and a tanker).

We have now arrived at a turning point in the history
of the convoys, resulting from a turn in war strategy.

While the PQ 18 and QP 14 were crossing these murderous waters, thousands of officers and civilians were pre-
paring the concentration of the Western Task Force
destined to invade North Africa. An enormous number of

warships were wanted for this operation. This was why at the end of September, 1942, the Allied Naval Command decided " no more escorts for the Arctic convoys." The official reason given was that now the days had drawn in the danger had also diminished.

Between the 29th October and the 2nd November, ten merchant ships (five British, five Americans) set sail in pairs for Reykjavik. The only protection given them was a few armed sloops spaced out along the route with orders to pick up survivors if possible. The crews thought this cover ridiculous and did not believe in the diminution of the danger. They shook hands with their pals as they left with bitter jokes about condemned men. Five of these ships reached port. One of them broke up on the ice pack and a few members of her crew were picked up. Nothing was ever heard of the other four.

Isolated ships were dispatched, also without escort, on the return journey—thirty ships from the end of October, 1942, to the 21st January, 1943. Only one of them was sunk. Obviously, the Germans were paying more heed to the ships sailing in the other direction. Moreover, the Admiralty statement turned out to be true: along a great part of the route the Arctic winter nights now protected the ships—at least against aircraft. The season for the hosts of torpedo-carrying aircraft and heavy bombers was over. Massive attacks comparable with those suffered by PQ 16, 17 and 18 would never be experienced again in the Arctic Ocean. But the struggle was far from over. It merely changed its aspects and the theatre of operations. The men in cargo boats and escort vessels had not yet finished suffering or losing their lives.

CHAPTER NINE

Operation Aurora

AT THE END OF 1942, THE GERMAN ARCTIC
zone of operations was placed under the orders of Admiral
Schniewind (Narvik), responsible to Admiral Carls, O.C.
Northern Theatre (Kiel), who in turn was responsible to
Grand Admiral Raeder (Berlin). This delegation of command was only semi-valid for the U-boats which, as has
already been mentioned, took their orders direct from
Admiral Doenitz at Lorient. For all these admirals, the
Arctic zone of operations was a great problem, one might
almost say a nightmare. The echoes and messages which
reached them, directly or not, from the Führer's H.Q.
expressed nothing but disappointment or displeasure. The
losses sustained by the Allied convoys on the Murmansk
run were far too low. The enthusiastic communiques issued
on " the massacred convoy " and the losses inflicted upon
the two subsequent convoys (PQ 18 and QP 13) must not
let one lose sight of the fact that, since the beginning of
the year, the convoys in the Arctic Ocean as a whole had
lost only fifty cargo ships out of 250. It was far too few.
Taking into account the means at the disposal of the
German naval command in Norway, the Führer maintained that it was ridiculous. The convoys got through at
the cost of losses which were quite acceptable to the Allies.
The crews in these Arctic convoys would probably have
been surprised to learn that someone considered their *via
dolorosa* as an outing. Opinions vary according to the
points of view. From a purely strategic point of view, a
fifth of the ships sunk was insufficient.

The displeasure shown by the Führer worried the German admirals all the more since winter made the use of aircraft almost impossible. Nor were the interminable nights and the storms favourable to the U-boats. There remained the surface ships ; the raiders. Since the beginning of the year, the *Tirpitz* (35,000 tons), the *Admiral Scheer* (pocket battleship, theoretically 10,000 tons), the *Admiral Hipper* (heavy cruiser, 10,000 tons) and the *Lützow* (ex-*Deutschland,* sister-ship of the *Admiral Scheer*) had followed each other to anchorage in the fjords. So far their activities had been far more potential than real. Their presence alone immobilised a part of the Home Fleet at Scapa Flow. They were an immobile but efficacious strategic factor, what the British called " a fleet in being." To their credit could be placed the fact that the tentative sortie of the *Tirpitz* at the beginning of July had caused the scattering of PQ 17 and its subsequent massacre. But now, unless they wished to see convoys get through all the winter with minor losses, it was essential that the surface ships should effectively intervene.

About 20th December, the Germans learned that the convoys for Russia were about to sail again. One of them was on the point of sailing from Loch Ewe.

In actual fact, the convoys had been resumed from the 15th December under new designations: the Russian-bound convoys were given the letters JW and the home-ward-bound RA. The JW and the RA were to follow a more southerly route than the PQ and QP because the ice-pack descended further south during the winter months. They did not touch at Iceland. They rounded and skirted the North Cape, the vast minefield between Scotland and Iceland, then made for Bear Island and Kola Inlet, the outer port of Murmansk.

The JW 51-A, the first of the series, sailed on the 15th September from Loch Ewe, reaching Kola Inlet ten days later, without loss or incident. The Germans only learned of its existence a few days after its arrival. Their agents informed them of the next sailing, which was JW 51-B. This was to become famous in the history of convoys.

A raiding force, consisting of the *Lützow*, the *Hipper* and six destroyers, lay with steam up at Narvik under the command of Admiral Kunmetz. Aerial reconnaissance patrols were sent into the North Atlantic and the Arctic. They were constantly relieved from 22nd December, despite the deterioration in the weather.

On Christmas Eve, the first message came from the aircraft, reporting the convoy with details of its position, route and strength: fourteen merchant ships escorted by six destroyers and five or six corvettes or sloops.

The order for " Operation Aurora " was immediately worked out, according to instructions from Berlin. This was the plan: the raiding force was to steal up on the convoy from astern. The *Hipper* was to show herself first and engage the destroyer escort, manoeuvring to invite their attack. The *Lützow* would then descend like a wolf upon the merchant ships and destroy them with her big guns. Nothing would then prevent her from approaching to sink the remainder, should there be any. This tactical plan having been approved by the High Command, Admiral Raeder telephoned his personal instructions to Kunmetz.

Kunmetz sailed with his ships, flying his flag in the *Hipper*.

On the 27th and 28th of November, other aircraft messages confirmed the strength of the convoy, which continued slowly on its way in very bad weather and in a wind approaching gale force.

On the 29th, a U-boat signalled: " Convoy sighted. Keeping contact." Kunmetz made a detour on an easterly course so as to surprise the convoy from astern, as arranged.

On the 31st December, about 08.00, between two of those snowfalls which made him fear that he would miss his prey, Kunmetz saw the convoy ahead. He immediately gave orders to begin the pincer movement. The *Hipper* veered to port to approach the convoy from the north, while the *Lützow* sailed south. " Operation Aurora " began in the most favourable conditions. The whole strategy of the German High Command had functioned without a hitch.

The information received by the Germans as to the strength of the convoy JW 51-B was accurate. Six destroyers (*H.M.S. Onslow, Orwell, Oribi, Obedient, Obdurate* and *Achates*) ; three corvettes (*H.M.S. Rhododendron, Hyderabad* and *Northern Gem*) ; two sloops (*H.M.S. Bramble* and *Vizalma*) escorted this convoy of fourteen merchant ships which had sailed on the 22nd September from Loch Ewe. Escort leader: *H.M.S. Onslow,* commanded by Captain Sherbrooke. Admiralty orders read that the JW 51-B was to have the support of the cruisers *H.M.S. Sheffield* and *Jamaica* which, having accompanied the preceding convoy to Kola Inlet, were to leave that port on the 27th for a fixed rendezvous on the 29th, at 73° N. and 11° E.

The merchant ships' crews were sorry to see only a few destroyers and other small escort vessels. They had no news of how JW 51-A had fared, and that they had the support of the cruisers ; they only knew that an escort consisting of an aircraft carrier, a cruiser, sixteen destroyers, two submarines and several corvettes and sloops had not prevented the PQ 18 from losing six ships. The briefness of daylight, the covered sky and the intermittent snowstorms were not enough to reassure them. Their fears increased when, on Christmas Day, the snow having ceased, a German recco plane flew over the convoy. The appearance of this first German spotter was now the classic sign which boded no good.

Christmas Day, however, passed without incident, as did Boxing Day. The 27th lulled the fears of these anxious crews.

The wind sprang up and increased in strength. It grew ever colder and the grey sea raged. On the morning of the 28th, an icy gale was blowing. There were eight inches of ice on the decks ; the ice entirely enveloped the hulls above the water line, the superstructure and the rigging ; the snow stuck and froze on this ice, forming a thick carapace; the fresh water pipes were all frozen. The convoy, completely dislocated, afforded a pathetic spectacle. Most of the cargo vessels had hove to or, reducing speed, steered so as to avoid the largest rollers. Several of them fell astern, apparently out of action. Captain Sherbrooke tried to sail west to round up the laggards, or at least to plot their exact positions, but there was such a high sea running that he had to give up. The destroyers tired perhaps more than the merchantmen ; their hulls rattled dangerously in these gigantic waves. The short daylight of the 28th and the night of the 28th/29th were spent in these conditions, each ship struggling individually in order to keep head on to the sea for fear of capsizing. The men on watch were swiftly transformed into blocks of ice and had to be relieved every hour.

At dawn on the 29th the wind fell a little and the situation looked less grim, but seven ships had disappeared: five merchant ships, the destroyer *H.M.S. Oribi* and the sloop *H.M.S. Vizalma*. Captain Sherbrooke ordered the *Bramble* to return westwards to try and find the stray ships. *H.M.S. Bramble* was a very solid sloop, carrying a large reserve of fuel. On receiving orders she put about and was soon lost to view behind a screen of snow. She was never seen again.

On the 30th, the snowfalls were at longer intervals. The convoy, reduced to nine cargo vessels and nine escorts, could continue on its easterly course in almost regular formation, in two columns. Neither the Commodore nor the Captain D knew its exact position. They thought that they must be somewhere between Jan Mayen Island and Bear Island. To imagine that the cruisers had turned up at the rendezvous would mean the risk of waiting a long time. Presumably they would not have waited. The only near certainty was that the convoy must now have reached a position within range of the enemy air bases. But the weather must have discouraged the aircraft, for none appeared. The storm had certainly not allowed the enemy to keep in contact by spotter after Christmas Day.

Night fell once more. In all the ships the look-outs scanned the darkness, for there was no indication that the U-boats were not still at sea. They could dive and escape the bad weather.

They had received no news of the stray ships.

At dawn on the 31st, the weather had improved considerably ; the sea had fallen and the wind had lost some of its violence, but it was strong enough at 20° below, to lash faces and bring tears to the eyes of the men on the frozen decks. Between the snowfalls, visibility increased to ten miles.

About 08.30 hours, *H.M.S. Obdurate* and the corvette *H.M.S. Hyderabad,* protecting the convoy to the south, suddenly saw two destroyers which at first they took for Russians.

(In principle, the Russian destroyers should have brought their support to the Allied escorts on leaving the seas round Bear Island. " It was agreed that they should do so," a British naval officer once told me. " Had they respected the arrangement it would have been a consolation for our lack of ' watchdogs.' We should have been less short of fuel ; in other words, we should have been more efficient and less vulnerable. But they never turned up at the rendezvous— never! By failing to do so they cost us a great deal.")

The two units sighted by the *Obdurate* and the *Hyderabad* cut the wake of the *Hyderabad* far astern, sailing north. The *Obdurate* reported to the *Onslow,* who gave her orders to go and identify the vessels. When the *Obdurate* arrived at about 6,000 yards from the presumed Russians, the gun flashes lit up the three grey shapes. They were firing on her. The identification was soon made.

The *Obdurate* put about at full speed to rally the convoy, sending the alarm to the escort leader, *Onslow.* But

Sherbrooke had already seen the flashes and heard the shots. He was on his way. In a flash he had assembled the *Obedient,* the *Orwell* and the *Obdurate,* and they were advancing at full speed on the enemy destroyers, while the *Achates* and the remaining escort vessels received orders to protect the convoy and to lay a smoke-screen.

It was now 09.30. Banks of fog dotted the grey surface of the sea and snow was falling in places. The four British destroyers plunged through these curtains, replying to the enemy's fire.

Suddenly at 09.41, dull deeper rumbles mingled with the noise of the destroyers' gunfire. Three waterspouts higher than the others rose from the sea. Less than a minute later, on the starboard bow, Sherbrooke saw the bulky silhouette of a warship which he identified at once as the *Hipper.*

Contrary to all his hopes, the convoy had not escaped the enemy reconnaissance. The *Hipper* was there with her eight 8-inch and her twelve 4-inch—without counting her destroyers' armament—and her speed of thirty-two knots. There was now every chance that the JW 51-B would take its place in the series of massacred convoys.

The crews of the cargo vessels had no idea of the danger that threatened them. They saw neither the *Hipper* nor the German destroyers: they all thought that the British destroyers had gone off to fire at aircraft.

On recognising the *Hipper,* Sherbrooke had not hesitated for a second: he continued to advance on the German cruiser with his flotilla. Without a moment's hesitation he conformed to the British naval tradition of engaging the enemy more closely.

Sherbrooke and his flotilla made for the *Hipper,* firing madly. Enormous waterspouts straddled the destroyers. Sherbrooke manoeuvred, weaving in a circle and coming in to E.N.E., but without retiring, each time drawing in closer to the adversary. The destroyers controlled their fire by radar, zig-zagging to confuse the *Hipper's* gunners.

They made feints as though to attack with torpedoes and then fired broadsides only to repeat the manoeuvre. We must not forget that this battle took place in an icy wind with snowstorms and squalls. There was always the fear of their guns freezing up. Fortunately for them, the *Hipper's* fire was hesitant and inaccurate. The moving curtains of snow hampered the cruiser as much as they hampered the destroyers. During the battle, Sherbrooke was thinking of the convoy, which the German destroyers were probably attacking. At 10.08, he despatched the *Obdurate* and the *Obedient* to rejoin the escorts and lead the convoy south, while the *Onslow* and the *Oribi* remained to keep the *Hipper* busy.

Although the German cruiser now had only two destroyers attacking, she did not seem anxious to close in. On the contrary, putting on speed, she veered north. Sherbrooke could not understand this behaviour, which to him smacked of cowardice. Was it possible?

In actual fact, Admiral Kunmetz was merely carrying out phase No. 1 of Operation Aurora: to lure the British destroyers away while the pocket battleship *Lützow* (six 11-inch and eight 6-inch guns) fell upon the convoy.

The cruisers H.M.S. *Sheffield* and *Jamaica,* under the command of Admiral Burnett, had left Kola Inlet on the 27th. Two days later they were at the rendezvous. The Admiral thought that the storm must have delayed the convoy, so he cruised about waiting for it.

At 09.31, as they were sailing north-west, his radar detected two ships dead ahead at 13,000 yards. These, he thought, must be the advance guard of the convoy. The cruisers put on speed.

But, oddly enough, as the distance diminished, the radar revealed no trace of ships in these waters. The two units detected were therefore presumed to be enemy craft and the alarm was sounded for action stations.

At 09.30, flashes were seen in the south. Good, thought the Admiral, the convoy must be over there. It's firing at aircraft. But let us first deal with these two suspects. A moment later, they had been identified as the sloop *Vizalma* accompanying a cargo vessel. Blown off their course by the storm of the 28th-29th, the two ships were heading independently for Kola Inlet. Burnett immediately put about on a southerly course in the direction of the gunfire. At that moment violent gunfire was heard and huge flashes cast a red glow against the snowy sky. At 09.40, a yeoman signaller handed the Admiral on the bridge Sherbrooke's message: "JW 51-B attacked by *Hipper* and several German destroyers." Burnett gave orders to increase speed to 31 knots.

The cruisers' hulls vibrated, the spray and waves flew over their bows; the gunners, with frozen faces, kept their guns constantly trained ahead. On the radar screens, the observers saw the distance separating the tiny spots, which were fighting warships, from the centre of the screen diminish very slowly. This distance was still about thirty miles.

The noise of the guns grew louder and the flashes increased in brilliance.

The *Onslow* and *Orwell* replied to the *Hipper's* fire. From the bridge of the *Onslow*, Captain Sherbrooke, his glasses to his eyes, watched with dismay the German cruiser which, although continuing to fire, was putting on speed and retreating. Suddenly, there was no more *Hipper* and no more destroyer. A terrible explosion and a blinding flash. . . . A salvo had just hit the *Onslow*. A column of flame rose from her stern. The funnel, split in two, rolled on the deck among steel splinters and the Captain lay on the bridge blinded in one eye. It was 10.10. Sherbrooke still had the strength to give his orders to all destroyers to rejoin the convoy and lay a smoke-screen. The first lieutenant immediately sent a signal to the *Obedient*, whose commander, Lieutenant-Commander Kinloch, was the senior officer in the flotilla. Kinloch automatically became Captain D.

The *Hipper* now concentrated her fire on the *Orwell*. The waterspouts straddled the destroyer. Her 4·7s continued to reply to the eight 8-inch guns, but it was obvious that this unequal battle could not last for more than a few minutes.

Suddenly, the shells ceased to fall and the guns fell silent. A whirling snowstorm had just descended upon the scene of action, reducing visibility to less than two miles.

The British destroyers could hardly see each other. The *Onslow*, minus a funnel, listing 15°, advanced like a phantom in the dim twilight. There were several dead on board. Sherbrooke had been taken to the sick bay badly wounded —according to the doctor probably fatally. To stern of the convoy, the *Achates*, which had received a direct hit, sent a signal " speed reduced to twelve knots."

The command which had fallen to Lieutenant-Commander Kinloch was a far from enviable one. The new Captain D found himself on an expanse of grey sea, limited by curtains of snow, with three able destroyers and two cripples, and a slow heavy convoy trailing southwards. Within range of the *Hipper* and her destroyers, all speedy and intact. From which beam would they now appear? How could he save the JW 51-B?

Kinloch gave orders to the *Onslow* and the *Achates* to take up their places, if they could, at the head of the convoy. He himself would take up a position with his able destroyers between the convoy and the probable position of the *Hipper*. There was only one possibility of still saving the convoy: for it to slip away with its escorts under the cover of darkness. The short polar day was drawing to a close. If the snow continued to fall until night there was a chance that the enemy might lose contact. In that case they would slip away and resume their course eastwards later.

If, on the other hand, the weather cleared before nightfall and the *Hipper* returned to the convoy, the only solution was to reply to the enemy's fire as long as possible.

Kinloch, of course, knew nothing of the clause in the orders "Operation Aurora" that the *Lützow* was to appear from the south.

Incredible though it may seem, the men in the convoy still did not know that they had been attacked by surface ships. They had not seen any. The smoke-screen laid by the destroyers had hidden the whole battle. They had only heard the gunfire, and still believed that their escorts were firing at planes.

The lull lasted twenty minutes.

At 11.00 the sea cleared to the north. The *Hipper* immediately opened fire. The men in the rear cargo vessels began to see enormous waterspouts around them and realised that their attackers were not aircraft. The *Hipper* was firing at the tail end of the convoy. Then she raised her sights and fired at the *Achates,* which could no longer zig-zag. Two shells hit the destroyer, making a breach in her hull, killing the Captain and forty ratings. She began to sink, drifting slowly, but continued to lay smoke to hide the convoy. Her agony lasted two hours.

Kinloch's three destroyers had also opened fire. The *Hipper,* having settled accounts with the *Achates,* replied from 7,000 yards. Kinloch tried to get into position for a torpedo attack. Impossible. The sea was too rough. The destroyers could not outstrip the cruiser. They had to resign themselves to an almost desperate battle with guns. The heavy cruiser suffered less from the sea than the destroyers and her ammunition would last much longer. There was a faint hope that darkness would arrive before they were destroyed, always supposing that their crews could bear the terrible strain imposed upon them. The cold had not diminished. The men slipped on the icy decks and the gunners were frozen and stabbed by the polar wind. In spite of these appalling conditions direct hits were obtained upon the *Hipper* but they did not seem to have any effect. She continued to fire unperturbed.

The diagrams show that between 11.10 and 11.25 the

German cruiser was following a south-westerly course, closing in on the destroyers, which were sailing south-east and then south. The distance diminished. Each of the destroyers was at the mercy of a single well-adjusted salvo from the eight-inch guns.

At 11.30, to the amazement of the British sailors, the *Hipper* broke off the action. She ceased fire, turned to starboard on a northerly course. Smoke was pouring from her stern. The destroyer crews were jubilant. The *Hipper* had been badly damaged and their direct hits had caused her to flee. This was the general conviction, which aroused great enthusiasm.

Gunflashes spurted once more from the cruiser's big turrets, but no shells fell around the *Obedient* and her two companions. So the *Hipper* was firing at another enemy.

A minute later a radio message from Admiral Burnett reached the destroyers. The cruisers *Sheffield* and *Jamaica* had arrived and had now engaged the *Hipper*. There were loud cheers. It mattered little that their fire had beaten off the German cruiser: the *Sheffield* and the *Jamaica* had arrived. An immense hope replaced their anxiety. In any case they had every reason to be well satisfied with themselves.

The *Obedient,* the *Orwell* and the *Obdurate* made off to resume their protection of the convoy. At that moment two salvoes, much more enormous than those of the *Hipper,* straddled the vessels at the rear of the convoy.

They were salvoes from the pocket battleship *Lützow.*

Burnett's cruisers had opened fire on the *Hipper* from 11,000 yards. The German cruiser was hit by the first salvoes. A thick black smoke rose from her stern. Through his glasses the Admiral could see that she had ceased to fire at the destroyers and put about like a large wild beast taken by surprise. Then new flashes from her guns. The *Hipper* had seen her new assailants and began to reply to their fire. But her firing was dispersed. The *Sheffield* and the *Jamaica* continued to fire at her as they zig-zagged.

At 11.33 the German cruiser disappeared in a squall and the exchange of shots ceased. At 11.37 the *Sheffield* saw a German destroyer ready to fire its torpedoes speed from a curtain of snow at 3,000 yards. The British cruiser immediately opened fire on this aggressor, the destroyer *Eckholdt*. Within three minutes it was transformed into a flaming hulk.

Aboard the two cruisers the radar operators followed the dot representing the *Hipper* on the luminous dial. This dot was moving away from the centre. The *Hipper,* having described a complete circle, was speeding at full speed to the west. The two cruisers pursued her at full speed in the failing light.

At 12.15 Admiral Burnett, between two squalls, saw a silhouette to the south-west which was not the *Hipper*. It was the *Lützow,* also sailing west. It disappeared almost immediately. A quarter of an hour later in another bright patch he distinguished the *Hipper* again. Burnett opened fire. She replied and at the same time the *Lützow* also reappeared. The flashes of her guns could be seen. As main armament the two units together disposed of six eleven-inch, eight eight-inch and eight six-inch. The eleven-inch guns of the *Lützow* could carry 32,000 yards. Her armour was that of a small battleship. The two light British cruisers had together twenty-four six-inch guns. The fight which was about to take place did not seem very equal.

Burnett made a detour to the north to deceive the enemy gunners and then veered west, but the two German ships were no longer visible ; ceasing their fire they both put on speed to the west and were swallowed up in the night.

The British cruisers continued to pursue them until 14.00. Radar observation showed that both the *Hipper* and the *Lützow* were increasing their lead. Burnett gave up the chase, made a detour with his ships to the south with the intention of covering the convoy should the two raiders reappear, but they had definitely thrown in their hand. Their " ghosts " had crossed the limits of the radar screen.

Not a single cargo vessel had been sunk in convoy JW 51-B.

And what of the *Lützow*? What happened to the *Lützow*? The pocket battleship completely " missed the boat." " Operation Aurora " ended in a bad setback.

According to plan, the pocket battleship had rounded the convoy from the south and passed a few miles ahead without seeing it. A providential snowstorm had momentarily masked it from view. Later, about midday, hearing the sound of the *Hipper's* guns engaged with Burnett's cruisers, the *Lützow* returned north-west. It was at this moment that she fired a few shells in the direction of Kinloch's destroyers. But without delay she joined the *Hipper* . . . to retire with her!

The German plan of attack had been ruined: Firstly, by the determined resistance or one might say offensive action of the destroyers under Sherbrooke's command and then under Kinloch.

Secondly, by the arrival of Burnett's cruisers. The behaviour of the British destroyers had given Burnett time to appear on the scene.

The result of the operation in plain English was as follows: A pocket battleship and a heavy cruiser escorted by six destroyers had not succeeded in destroying a single vessel of a convoy protected by six British destroyers and ultimately rescued by two light cruisers. The two raiders and their escorts had fled before a naval force considerably inferior to their own. This tactical setback was a great blot on the German Navy.

Commandant Vulliez who knew and questioned Sherbrooke, and who from perusing the British and German reports has accurately reconstructed the action of this engagement on Christmas Day, 1942, has clearly shown the reasons for the German setback. The personal instructions given by Grand Admiral Raeder to Kunmetz before he sailed were as follows: "Don't take too many risks." The *Hipper* and the *Lützow* were valuable units and irreplaceable. There was no sense in risking them to sink a few cargo ships. Kunmetz therefore put to sea with an *idée fixe*: not to risk his big units. The orders given to his destroyers were formal: their task was protection. Thus they were not allowed to take the least initiative. As a matter of fact we have seen that the German destroyers only intervened once ; against the British cruisers, to protect the *Hipper*.

As soon as Kunmetz learned that the *Lützow* had missed the convoy to the south, he still had an opportunity of bringing "Operation Aurora" to a victorious conclusion. Sweeping from the north with his destroyers he could have cleared the board. He did not fail to do this from lack of courage but in order to conform to strict orders. Moreover, the behaviour of Sherbrooke and then Kinloch had impressed him ; on several occasions the *Hipper* took evasive action to avoid imaginary torpedoes. The *Hipper* thus remained north of the convoy instead of attacking during those three hours when his only adversaries were four destroyers and then only three—and when he knew that the *Lützow* was on his beam a few miles to the south. But he was not allowed to expose either of these big units to danger.

The orders given by Raeder to Kunmetz were only the result of personal orders given by the Führer. Hitler was furious to see that his big warships won no victories and were as he said "useless," yet he was scared to risk them. He had an almost pathological fear of the loss of prestige that another loss of a capital ship like the *Graf Spee* would have been. This fear had even made him change the name of the *Deutschland* to the *Lützow* ; in no circumstances was a ship bearing the name of *Deutschland* to be sunk. That would have been intolerable. . . . Moreover, a further loss of a capital ship would have been disastrous. For sailors to act in this way meant that there were none left! The result of these orders had been to paralyse them as soon as an operation entailing the big units was planned: "What they feared in the German Navy was not combat but the wrath of their Führer," Commandant Vulliez says quite correctly. "They trembled not only before the thunder of the British guns but before the voice of Hitler asking for an account rendered." A setback such as that incurred by "Operation Aurora" was the logical result of this state of mind.

The final balance of the operation was as follows: One destroyer sunk, *H.M.S. Achates,* 81 survivors. One destroyer damaged, *H.M.S. Onslow.* She reached Kola Inlet to land her wounded and to undergo indispensable repairs. One sloop lost, *H.M.S. Bramble.*

We have already seen the sloop *Vizalma* escorting a cargo vessel on the way to Kola Inlet. The two ships arrived safely after having risked for a few moments being shelled by Admiral Burnett's cruisers.

The destroyer *H.M.S. Oribi* which disappeared in the storm of the 28th reached Kola Inlet on the 31st, without having been able to find the convoy.

The four other cargo ships that were blown off their course in the gale all managed to reach Kola Inlet. The last was a Panamanian which arrived on the 5th January after being refloated from the ice-pack where she had beached. Thus not a single ship of the convoy was lost.

Hardly had the majority of the convoy reached port than Winston Churchill spoke on the radio to announce this naval victory. Stressing the inequality of the forces engaged, he extolled the courage of the destroyer crews with the natural brilliance and eloquence he always displays when speaking of valour.

Captain Sherbrooke was awarded the V.C.

The German communications functioned badly. Hitler did not hear the result of "Operation Aurora" until some time later—actually from the voice of the British Prime Minister. He immediately summoned Admiral Krancke,

Naval Attaché at his G.H.Q., and sent insulting reproaches to Grand Admiral Raeder and the whole German Navy. A few days later, when Raeder arrived at G.H.Q. with full reports of the action, the Führer would not even let him speak. He himself raved for more than an hour, heaping abuse on the head of his Naval chief before all the assembled staff officers. In conclusion he ordered the Admiral to prepare the scrapping of all the surface units and to suggest dates for the dismantling of their big guns.

Raeder, refusing to accept this sentence, wrote a memo in defence of the surface fleet. His plea receiving no reply, the Admiral resigned.

CHAPTER TEN

Operation Source

THE ARCTIC AND THE ANTARCTIC SEAS ARE the most inhospitable in the world. The vicinity of the Pole upsets magnetic compasses. In winter the darkness and the snowstorms reduce visibility to almost nil. The wind blows at gale force sometimes more than 100 m.p.h. The waves crash down upon the ships like hammer blows sometimes swamping the funnels and putting out the fires in the boilers.

If these conditions were appalling for the crews of the ships despatched from Scotland they were hardly more agreeable for the German airmen ordered to attack the convoys. The machines ready to take off from the Norwegian airfields had to be secured by steel cables to cement blocks weighing a ton. Each take off was in the nature of a feat. And yet, after the setback to the *Hipper* and the *Lützow* against convoy JW 51-B, both aircraft and U-boats were sent to play their part.

At the outset the attack always followed the same pattern. The recco plane sighted the convoy and the bombers were sent up. But their task was infinitely harder than it had been in the summer. The shortness of the days allowed no waste of time, no errors in navigation ; the attackers flew towards the target in storms and snow squalls and were lucky if they ever caught sight of it. The wind which had lashed them on their approach flight was inclined to make them drift at the decisive moment of the attack. Of the dozen aircraft which took off on the 24th January to attack convoy JW 52 (thirteen cargo vessels, a score of destroyers and small escorts) only three reached the convoy. They pressed home their attack in the squall beneath the concentrated ack-ack fire. All three were shot down. The JW 52 reached Kola Inlet without loss. The following convoy, JW 53 (twenty-two cargo vessels, a cruiser, twenty other escort vessels of which eleven were destroyers), also reached Kola Inlet without loss. The attacking aircraft were never able to approach their target. However, the orders from Berlin were categorical: "Attack the convoy irrespective of the weather." The RA 53 (thirty cargo ships, twenty-five escort vessels, including three cruisers and eleven destroyers) was attacked five times during the course of 5th March by aircraft and U-boats. The submarines sank a cargo ship at 09.30. At 14.30 a dozen dive-bombers appeared but none of them could penetrate the ack-ack barrage. Unfortunately the RA 53 met another enemy: the foulest winter weather. The liberty ship *J. L. M. Curry* was smashed by the heavy seas. The crews of the other ships to their horror saw her lifted by a colossal wave and break in two. Her crew was rescued. The storm separated many ships of this convoy. Twenty-two arrived together at Loch Ewe and then four more in succession. The remainder were lost at sea. The *Richard Bland* received a torpedo from a submarine, invisible in the heavy seas. Twenty of her crew were drowned and the remainder rescued. The *Puerto Rican* was torpedoed and sunk on 9th March, 280 miles from Iceland. The lifeboats, frozen to their davits, could not be lowered. From a crew of sixty-two only eight managed to climb aboard a raft. All except one were swept off by the waves or perished in the cold. The sole survivor, a stoker, was picked up on the 12th March by a British destroyer. He was half crazed and three parts dead. The military doctors at Reykjavik could not understand how he had survived. Both his feet had to be amputated.

After the voyage of the RA 53, the danger from the air becoming greater with the arrival of the longer days, the

Admiralty sent less and less convoys by the Arctic route. The Allies had regained control of the Mediterranean and the war supplies destined for Russia could now use the route Gibraltar-Suez-Persian Gulf.

Nevertheless the northern route was not yet entirely abandoned. It was for this reason, among others, that afraid of seeing the traffic grow more intense, the German High Command kept its large units in the Norwegian fjords. The presence of this " fleet in being " which immobilised part of the Home Fleet at Scapa Flow was a perpetual thorn in the side of the Admiralty. For a long time—in actual fact since the spring of 1942—the Admiralty had planned to rid itself of these powerful raiders by attacking them at anchorage with midget submarines. The plan was officially known as " Operation Source."

The results of this operation were announced by the B.B.C. in September, 1943. The details of its preparation and the action were not known in Great Britain until 1947 after the official reports of Rear-Admiral C. B. Barry, D.S.O., C.-in-C. Submarines, and of the commanders of the midget submarines had been published. This is the tale of Operation Source reconstructed from the official documents.

On the 12th May, 1942, a contract was signed with Messrs. Vickers Armstrong Ltd. for the building of six submarines of a new type.

At this period two prototypes of midget submarines existed, X3 and X4. It is impossible to know for what operation they had been intended. All the great navies of the world have constantly planned or built secret ships of apparatus.

At the same time as this contract was signed, volunteers were called for submarine ratings " to undertake a bold and dangerous mission." The training of these selected men in the prototypes X3 and X4 began shortly after this in the greatest secrecy.

The six midget submarines ordered were delivered on

31st December, 1942, and 16th January, 1943. Here are their chief characteristics: thirty feet overall length and displacement of ten tons (?). They could sail at between four and five knots on the surface and more slowly when submerged. Even when surfaced they were almost invisible, because their deck lay very low in the water, and they possessed a very short mast in place of a conning tower. Their armament was neither a torpedo nor, of course, a gun. Fixed to each side of their hull they carried very powerful charges of explosive with a time fuse which had to be placed beneath the target. Their crew consisted of an officer and four specialised ratings.

Even today the remaining specifications of these ships are still a secret. None of them returned after Operation Source.

The attack against the battleships was planned for the spring of 1943, before the period when the nights became too short. The extreme date envisaged was 9th March, 1943, but it was soon apparent that this short delay would not allow time for the training of the crews and to get the vessels in fighting trim. This problem turned out to be harder than anticipated.

Another problem arose which was not easily solved: how to transport the midgets near to the targets. Several methods were tried before it was discovered that the best method was to have them towed by ordinary submarines. On 11th February, 1943, Admiral Barry informed the First Sea Lord that the operation would have to be postponed until the autumn.

On the 17th April, 1943, the 12th Submarine Flotilla was formed under the orders of Captain W. E. Banks " to group the special weapons and to co-ordinate their training." The officer directly responsible for this training was Commander D. C. Ingram. Rear-Admiral Barry supervised the preparation of the whole operation.

From 4th July the " Xs " delivered by Vickers, having completed their trials, joined the depot ship *Bonaventure* at Loch Cairnbawn, north of Loch Ewe. It was referred to in secret documents as port HHZ. The real training began. A battleship detailed for the purpose served as target.

At the same time the planning continued under the direction of Commander G. P. S. Davies.

To attack they had to wait for the nights to draw out again ; but they could not wait too long lest the bad weather in autumn should seriously interfere with the operation. Moreover, it was necessary to take into account the moon whose light would enable the " Xs " to find their way through the fjords. The period 20-25th September was chosen during which the moon was in its last quarter. " J Day," when the midget submarines were to be shipped by their big brothers at a spot within striking distance of the targets was set provisionally for 20th September.

Information given by aircraft showed that the German capital ships changed their moorings from time to time. It was therefore necessary to organise the operation in such a manner that they could be attacked wherever they lay. Three alternatives of Operation Source corresponding to three different zones were therefore planned.

1. North of parallel 70° N ; variation Funnel.
2. Between parallels 67° and 69° ; variation Empire.
3. Between parallels 63° and 65° ; variation Forced.

It was essential to organise the photographic reconnaissance to obtain last-minute information in order to see which variation should be used. Now the most northerly zone, Alten Fjord, was out of range of the British recco planes. On the 12th May, the C.-in-C. Home Fleet proposed that the British personnel charged with the aerial reconnaissance should be sent to Northern Russia. Negotiations with the invariably suspicious Soviet authorities were rather laborious. Nevertheless the despatch of aircraft and staff to Murmansk was finally authorised.

On the 27th August, the destroyers *H.M.S. Musketeer* and *Mahratta* left the Faroe Islands with the R.A.F. photographic staff and provisions. They arrived at Murmansk on the 31st. On 3rd September, three Spitfires arrived at Vaenga airfield near Murmansk. They made their first flight on the 7th. Despite their efforts the first aerial photos only arrived in Great Britain a few hours before the submarines put to sea. All the details as to the positions of the enemy battleships and the obstacles were obtained by Russian recco aircraft and sent to Operation Source before the submarines left.

It was decided that the flotilla of submarines should sail direct from Loch Cairnbawn for the operation. On 30th August the submarine depot ship *Titania* relieved the *Bonaventure*. Next day and on the 1st September, the following submarines arrived at Loch Cairnbawn: *H.M.S. Thrasher, Truculent. Stubborn, Syrtis, Sceptre* and *Seanymph,* specially equipped to tow the " X " craft. Two other submarines similarly equipped, *H.M.S. Satyr* and *Seadog,* were held in reserve at Scapa Flow twenty-four hours' sailing time away.

Two crews had been formed for each midget submarine: one to take her across and the second to replace it for the actual operation. This was so that the men carrying out the attack should be relaxed and fresh.

Special rigorous security measures had been taken at Loch Cairnbawn. No leave was granted to the ratings in this port and with the exception of a few officers they were only allowed to go ashore within very prescribed limits. All other ships except those engaged in Operation Source were kept in port until the signal " Operation ended " had been received.

On 3rd September a Soviet recco plane reported that the *Tirpitz,* the *Scharnhorst* and the *Lützow* were in the zone of Alten Fjord—northern-most zone. Variation Funnel was therefore chosen.

After a reconnaissance on the 7th the Spitfires reported: " Only the *Lützow* present." The *Tirpitz* and the *Scharnhorst* had been spotted off Ice Fjord, Spitzbergen. Further information received on the 10th: " *Tirpitz* and *Scharnhorst* have returned to Alten Fjord." The same evening the Russians confirmed: *Tirpitz* and *Scharnhorst* alongside the quay at Kaa Fjord (a branch of Alten Fjord). On the other hand, no *Lützow*.

On 11th September Rear-Admiral Barry arrived at Loch Cairnbawn. The following day he informed the C.-in-C. Home Fleet that he intended to carry out Operation Source, variation Funnel. " J Day " was 20th September. The submarine flotilla put to sea during the next two days in the following order: 11th September, 16.00: *Truculent* and X6, *Syrtis* and X9 ; 18.00: *Thrasher* and X5 ; 20.00: *Seanymph* and X8 ; 21.00: *Stubborn* and X7 ; 12th September, 13.00: *Sceptre* and X10. The operational crews were aboard the towing submarines. The sailing crews were aboard the " Xs."

The crossing was made without incident from the 11th to the 14th September. The full-sized submarines sailed on the surface, each towing their " X " below the surface. It is obvious that the latter had to be hidden at all costs until the attack. The memory of the midget submarines used by the Japanese at Pearl Harbour (not to attack but to get information) was still fresh in people's minds. The discovery of these midgets would have given the alert to the German High Command far more quickly than the sight of any capital ship. Although several incidents forced the " Xs " to sail on the surface, as we shall see, they were never spotted by the enemy.

Three or four times in twenty-four hours the " Xs " surfaced for air. The crews of the towing submarines watched the appearance of these tiny bobbins with the greatest interest. They had already got used to seeing them but the idea of these toy craft going in to deliver such an audacious attack still intrigued them.

The latest aerial reconnaissance reports from Great Britain were transmitted in code to the expedition: the

Tirpitz and *Scharnhorst* were still tied up at Kaa Fjord, the *Lützow* was at anchor in another creek of Alten Fjord —Lange Fjord. The plan of attack No. 4 was adopted: the X5, X6 and X7 were to place their explosives charges under the *Tirpitz*; the X9 and X10 under the *Scharnhorst*; the X8 would place hers under the *Lützow*.

On 15th September just after 04.00, the Captain of the X8, towed at eight knots by *Seanymph*, noticed that his craft had stopped. She surfaced; no *Seanymph* to be seen in the grey morning light. At 04.30, X8 set out alone on the surface: at three knots, course 29°. A heavy sea was soon running and the small craft was badly buffeted.

It was not until 06.00, the hour that the X8 normally surfaced for air, that the Captain of the *Seanymph* noticed that his charge was no longer in tow. He put about immediately on course 209°. The wind was blowing S.S.E., the sky was overcast and there was a heavy sea running.

We must now follow this crossing as closely as possible. It was not to take place without further incidents and not without tragedy.

15th September, 15.50—The Captain of the X7, towed by *Stubborn*, noticed that the towline had broken. He surfaced immediately, A new towline was passed.

16.30—The X8, sailing alone, saw the *Stubborn* team. It approached and made contact.

17.18—The *Stubborn* with X7 in tow and X8 nearby set out to find the *Seanymph*. She was not found.

19.00—Dusk. *Stubborn*, X7 and X8 sailed north.

19.54—*Stubborn* reported the situation in code to Admiral Barry.

21.57—*Seanymph*, which had looked in vain for X8 and reported its disappearance to Admiral Barry, received a reply informing her that X8 was with the *Stubborn*, and giving her the course. *Seanymph* set her course to intercept them.

23.05—*Stubborn* noticed that X8 was no longer in their company. The small craft had disappeared.

16th September, 03.15—Dawn, *Stubborn* spotted a submarine which she identified as *Seanymph*, position: 69° 35′ N., 10° 16′ E. 160 miles N.N.W. of Narvik. Information passed to *Seanymph,* who was looking for her baby.

09.07—*Syrtis*, towing X9, fired three submarine signal charges to attract the attention of her small charge that the hour for ventilation had long passed. No reaction. At 09.20 she hauled on the tow line ; it was broken. *Syrtis* put about. By examining the fuel consumption graph she calculated that the X9 must have ceased to be in tow from some time between 01.45 and 03.00.

15.45—*Syrtis* discovered an oily patch on the sea flowing from west to east, probably from an " X ". The route west-east was the direct course towards the slipping point 200 miles away. The search brought no further result. The X9 was never heard of again.

Once more the sea would guard her secret for ever.

17.00—*Seanymph* at last saw X8 sailing alone on the surface. Fortunately, the sea was now calmer. At 20.00, the small craft was in tow again. The Captain of the *Seanymph,* thinking that it was prudent to take advantage of the good weather, ordered the transfer of the X8 crews to take place without delay.

On the following morning, mechanical troubles started in the X8. The air was escaping from the starboard explosive charge. (These floats were calculated to reduce the weight of the charges to nil while they remained attached to the midget submarine.) At 16.00, the Captain of the X8 was forced to admit that the weight of the charge was endangering his craft. He decided to jettison it. He set the pointer at "Safety" and jettisoned the explosive at 16.35. Four minutes later, a violent explosion rocked the X8 900 yards from the spot where it had been jettisoned; it had exploded despite the safety position.

The explosion caused no damage but the X8 continued to have trouble with her steering. She had a list to port which grew more and more pronounced. It was obvious that the port float was now leaking too. The craft threatened to capsize ; the Captain jettisoned the other charge at 17.52 after setting the fuse at two hours delay. At 18.40, the X8, three and a half miles away, heard the charge explode. She was badly shaken and damaged. Her ballast tanks were bent and the pipes broken. X8, no longer able to attack, having no charges left, was now unable to dive.

The 17th September, " J3 " day, was the day when, according to plans, the midget submarines' crews were to be transferred. The weather, which in the morning had not been particularly favourable for the manoeuvre, now grew worse. The wind blew strongly from the south-east and a heavy sea was running. The transfer had to be delayed.

On the 18th at dawn, the Captain of X8 reported his engine trouble to the *Seanymph*. The latter decided to take off the sailing crew and to scuttle the craft. (On the 16th a message from Admiral Barry had given him permission to do this in case of emergency.) At 03.45 the X8 was sunk at 71° 41′ N., 18° 11′ E. The *Seanymph* set a northerly course to report to Admiral Barry by radio. (Transmissions had to be reduced to a minimum below 73° N.)

0.55—*Syrtis,* having reported the loss of X9, set her course for her patrol zone, *i.e.,* where she was to wait the return of the X craft after the attack.

20.15—The weather having slightly improved, the Captain of the *Stubborn* ordered the transfer of the attacking crew on board the X7. The others (*Truculent* with X6, *Thrasher* with X5 and *Sceptre* with X10, considered the weather too bad to attempt the transfer.)

21.28—*Stubborn* broke her tow line as she got under way. It was the spare line, since the other had snapped on the 17th. She had to make a jury line. She could not leave with X7 in tow until 01.25 on the 19th.

19th September, 08.55—Rear-Admiral Barry received the message from the *Seanymph* reporting the scuttling of the X8. The Admiral decided that this submarine should be used for intercepting any enemy units the attack might drive out of the fjords. *Seanymph* received the appropriate orders. The news of the scuttling of the X8 was not communicated to the other submarines in order not to weaken the morale of the crews. As for the news of the loss of the X9, it never reached Great Britain. The message from *Syrtis* was never received. The Admiral only learned of it on 3rd October.

The weather having improved, *Thrasher*, *Truculent* and *Sceptre* successfully transferred their crews and proceeded on their way without incident.

20th September, " J " day, 01.05—At 70° 45' N., 21° 03' E. (thirty miles from Stjernö Island at the entrance to Alten Fjord) the *Stubborn* towing X7 on the surface met a floating mine. She just avoided it but the mine caught in the tow line and floated almost to the bows of X7. The danger was immediate. The *Stubborn* stopped.

The mine was there—a large black object visible on the surface in the moonlight. The sailors in the *Stubborn* could see it clearly stuck between the tow line and the hull of the X7, rising and falling against the hull. A slightly larger wave had only to arrive for the horns to break and the mine to have exploded.

A figure appeared on the narrow deck of the X7. It was Lieutenant Place, the Captain. He made his way to the bows and pushed the mine gently away with his foot. It slipped away to stern. A general sigh of relief . . . The *Stubborn* got under way.

03.00—The *Syrtis* spotted a surfaced submarine and recognised her for a German. (The identification of enemy warships by a mere glance at their silhouettes was an important part of naval training in wartime. A submarine officer could recognise almost without hesitation the shapes of friendly or enemy vessels.) In accordance with orders the *Syrtis* did not attack. All ships participating in " Opera-

179

tion Source " had been given orders to attack no unit smaller than a battleship.

When day broke, the Norwegian coast was in sight. The weather continued to improve during the course of the day ; a moderate south-easterly breeze, calm sea, visibility good. Between 18.30 and 20.00, *Thrasher, Truculent, Stubborn* and *Sceptre* slipped their midgets. The small craft now continued on the way independently. The big submarines retired to their patrol zones where they were to wait for the return of the Xs. All those which left for the attack were in good mechanical order with the exception of X10, whose periscope hoisting motor and ballast pump were functioning badly. " The operational crew of the X10 eagerly desired to be in the action despite these difficulties. It was hoped to repair them or to find a make-shift."

According to the plan of operations, the X5, X6 and X7 were to attack the *Tirpitz*. The X9 having been lost, the X10 was to attack the *Scharnhorst* on her own. Since the X8 had been scuttled, the *Lützow* would not be attacked.

The German battleships were anchored at the end of the fjord. Between them and the attackers, obstacles had been placed at about forty miles: mine fields, booms and anti-torpedo nets. A boom carrying one of these nets closed the entrance to the fjord. In addition to this, each battle-ship was protected by its individual net. Cutters patrolled the fjords. Their hydrophones could pick up any suspicious sounds. The midgets would have to deal with all these defences. From now on they were acting independently. We shall now follow the journey of the X10, commanded by Lieutenant Hudspeth.

Although the interior structure of these X craft has remained a military secret, we can have some idea of the crew's conditions: they must have been exceedingly un-comfortable. The engines and various apparatus took nearly all the space and the men hardly had room to move. Each man was constantly at his post, the Captain above the others, his eyes glued to his periscope. The practical impossibility of moving about, the necessity not to relax vigilance for an instant was a heavy ordeal, apart from the dangers they were running. The air soon grew thick. The food consisted of concentrates and a few drugs to reduce to a minimum the demands of the poor human bodies. Naturally, no sleep.

20th September, 20.00[1]—X10 slipped by the *Sceptre* at 70° 41′ N., 21° 07′ E. After a trial dive, surfaced and sailed at full speed through the minefield. No incident.

23.00—Recognised the entrance to Stjernstund (a reach south of Stjernö Island) at a distance of twenty miles.

21st September, 02.05—The X10 dived five miles from the west point of Stjernö. Almost immediately the gyro-compass ceased to function. Periscope hoisted. The hoisting motor functioning worse and worse, the Captain decided to make for a neighbouring fjord to repair these breakdowns. An attack would be impossible in these conditions.

07.00—The X10 came to rest on the sandy bottom at the end of Smalfjord. The day was spent in repairs.

17.50—The repairs being adequate but rather precarious, the X10 surfaced and left her haven, skirting the shore. At 21.35, a fishing vessel was sighted, carrying navigation lights.

23.20—Entered Alten Fjord. The Captain decided to penetrate Kaa Fjord (where the *Tirpitz* and the *Scharnhorst* were) the following morning at dawn. Set their course south, skirting the east coast.

22nd September, 01.10—The gyro-compass ceased to function. Navigation was carried out as well as possible by the magnetic compass (uncertain).

01.35—Ship sighted ahead showing navigation lights. X10 dived.

01.50—Breakdown of the lighting of the magnetic compass. Surfaced to periscope depth. At the moment of sur-

1. Greenwich Mean Time. Add two hours thirty minutes to get the local time. This applies to all the times given in this account.

facing, the hoisting engine caught fire. The submarine filled with smoke and the men were suffocated. She surfaced for air almost at the entrance to Kaa Fjord.

The cliffs of the fjord were outlined against a misty moonlit sky. All was quiet at the approaches. Lieutenant Hudspeth, on the deck of his midget submarine, stared gloomily at this desolate scene. He knew that for him an attack was impossible. The X10 could not go into action with neither periscope nor compass; she would not even be able to dive and approach the *Scharnhorst*. He took the most difficult decision he had had to take in his career: he told his crew that they would have to abandon Operation Source.

On 22nd September at 02.15, the X10 settled once more on the sandy bottom four and a half miles from the entrance to Kaa Fjord. The crew made a further attempt to repair the compass.

08.30—Two loud explosions were heard. The ship's company of the X10 looked at each other without a word. This was the moment when, according to plan, the other submarine would be making their attack. At 08.35, nine explosions further off rang out at short irregular intervals.

" They must have pulled it off," said the commander of the X10. " So much the better."

The crew knew nothing of the scuttling of the X8 or the loss of the X9. The four men were convinced that all the other X craft had carried out their missions.

After remaining the whole day on the bottom, the X10 surfaced at 18.00 on 22nd September and set course for the open sea. The damage had not been repaired. She managed to rejoin her large sisters and was taken in tow by the *Stubborn*—at 01.50 on the 29th, a week later! The detailed account of the X10's return is an adventure story on its own. The crew which had been obliged to give up Operation Source sought the towing submarines in vain in a heavy sea swept by snow storms. She returned to shelter in a deserted fjord, managed to repair the faulty compass, set sail again and crossed the minefields, patrolled without catching sight of a friendly ship, returned to the haven of Sörö Island where the crew waited two days in an empty bay. The entrance to Alten Fjord was only forty miles away and yet the men might have been 4,000 miles from a war or even from a human being. The snow covered the banks of the fjord and the hull of their tiny craft. At last they put to sea again and found the *Stubborn*. The X10 received the congratulations she deserved.

No news of the other midget submarines. After waiting in vain for the X5, X6 and X7, *Thrasher*, *Truculent*, *Syrtis* and *Stubborn*—the latter having the X10 in tow—headed for home. On the 3rd October, at 17.00, the Met having issued a gale warning, Rear-Admiral Barry sent a message to the *Stubborn* to re-embark the crew of the X10 and, if she could not continue to tow her without danger, to scuttle her. The order was carried out at 20.40. The X10 disappeared beneath the waves at 66° 13′ N., 4° 02′ E. The submarines returned to port without a single one of their charges.

The Admiralty, however, knew that Operation Source had not been a failure. On the 24th September, a reconnaissance aircraft reported that the *Tirpitz* was still at her moorings in the fjord. She had a heavy list and was surrounded by a patch of oil flowing downstream on the fjord waters for a distance of two miles.

It was only eighteen months later, when Lieutenants Cameron and Place returned from a prisoner-of-war camp and told their story, that the full details of Operation Source were known. The story of these officers tallied with German documents seized, particularly the log book of the *Tirpitz*.

But let us return to the 20th September, 1943. The four midget submarines X5, X6, X7 and X10 were slipped between 18.30 and 20.00. They crossed the minefields, surfaced. We know the fate of the X10: let us follow the others.

At 23.15, the X7 exchanged good luck signals and good hunting with the X5. The latter sailed off and we shall not see her again.

The X6 (Lieutenant D. Cameron) and X7 (Lieutenant B. C. G. Place) dived between 01.45 and 02.15 on the 21st. A little later, the X7 had to manoeuvre to avoid several ships. The Captain of X6 noticed a fault in his periscope, but she was able to continue, still below the surface.

At 12.45, he came up for air and dived just in time to avoid being spotted by a German patrol vessel.

At 16.30, the Captain of the X7 spotted a large unit at anchor, presumably the *Scharnhorst,* but her target was the *Tirpitz.*

At nightfall the two X craft reached their waiting positions at the entrance to Kaa Fjord. The first hours of the night slipped by. The Captain of the X6 noticed that the clocks of his explosive charges were wrong. He blocked their mechanism at one hour delay.

Dawn of the 22nd September broke. The X7 made her way towards the boom which sealed the entrance to Kaa Fjord. The gate was open and X7 entered the fjord. X6 followed in her wake at 05.05.

(At Pearl Harbour the Japanese midget submarines had entered the port in exactly the same conditions. The boom gates had to be opened frequently to allow small patrol or surface vessels to pass. It was a long and tricky manoeuvre: when two ships had to pass at a short interval, the skipper of the tug who opened the gate usually left it open between these two passages.)

No suspicion was aroused aboard the *Tirpitz.* The action stations call was given at the usual hour and the gunners made their way leisurely to their posts.

After crossing the boom, the X7 sailed below the surface in the direction of the *Tirpitz,* but she was suddenly pulled up with a jolt: she had just run into the anti-submarine net protecting the *Lützow* (absent).

The X6 had trouble with her periscope. The Captain gave orders to dive to four fathoms to clean it, continuing to advance by dead reckoning towards the *Tirpitz* ; then he surfaced to periscope depth. He found that he was a few yards away from the German tanker *Nordmark* and manoeuvred just in time to avoid its mooring buoy. Immediately, the periscope was flooded and the brake of the hoisting engine caught fire. Would the X6 have to give up as the X10 had done? For the moment it continued on its course, nearly blind, towards the *Tirpitz*.

For more than an hour the X7 had been trying to disentangle herself from the *Lützow's* net. A pump was out of action as well as the gyro-compass. At last, at 06.00, they were free. They made for the *Tirpitz* at periscope depth. The Captain decided to pass under the *Tirpitz's* net.

07.10—Set the two charges at one hour's delay and descended to twelve fathoms. A jolt. The X7 was caught in the net.

For three minutes (at 07.07), the X6 had been spotted. Sailing blind towards the *Tirpitz,* she foundered. In an effort to refloat, she surfaced and a look-out man in the German battleship caught sight of her for a few seconds.

The sailor reported to the officer on watch: " Long object resembling a submarine." Even with little experience of military hierarchies, it is easy to imagine that a report furnished by an ordinary rating in these conditions would hardly provoke an immediate reaction. The sailor was doubted and interrogated in detail. This waste of time was all to the advantage of the midget submarine.

The X6 surfaced at seventy yards from the *Tirpitz.* Opening the hatch, the Captain saw the enormous vessel. He closed the hatch at once and dived. Without hesitation, he made straight for the enemy ship. There was no need of a periscope to reach such a close target. Five minutes later she was caught, as the X7 had been, in the battleship's submarine net, but by reversing engines she managed to free herself.

On board the *Tirpitz* it was finally decided to believe the report of the look-out man. At 07.20 the watertight compartments were closed and the crew was called to action stations. The preliminary orders for sailing were given, but, since the boilers had not sufficient steam up, the *Tirpitz* could not leave its nets for several hours. A few destroyers with steam up sailed at full speed and began dropping depth charges all over the fjord.

The X6 had freed herself but had been obliged to surface on the port bow of the *Tirpitz,* a few yards away: too close to be fired at either by the guns or the heavy ack-ack.

But she was raked by machine-guns, and the German sailors flung hand-grenades at her. The X6 dived, reversed engines until her stern grazed the hull of the *Tirpitz.* Every second was now precious. The Captain and the crew hastily destroyed their secret gear and the two explosive charges, set at an hour's delay, were jettisoned. The mission had been carried out.

The X6, shaken by the shock, could no longer remain below the water. She surfaced alongside the *Tirpitz* a few yards from a German launch. It sped towards her. The Captain had just time to scuttle his ship. A few seconds later he was taken prisoner with his crew. The German launch tried in vain to take the X6 in tow as it sank. Everything had happened in a flash.

Now a scene took place which might be called honourable from a human standard. It was one of those comforting exceptions which become ever rarer in our increasingly total wars.

Lieutenant Cameron and his companions were prisoners aboard the *Tirpitz.* They were interrogated by the German officers but the documents give no details of these interrogations. It is obvious that the crew of the X6 refused to give any information as to how they had arrived at the target, but the Germans could not fail to recognise the essential facts and to know that the men before them had carried out an extraordinary exploit by penetrating with their midget submarine to the heart of the German defences with intent to destroy or damage the *Tirpitz*.

But although the crew of the X6 refused to be explicit, the Germans were in no doubt as to the nature of their attack: German documents prove that they guessed correctly that explosive charges had been dropped. Moreover, the German reaction took shape: the boom was closed—a trifle late! The battleship was hauled by hawsers attached to the quayside to try and change her position and remove her from the dangerous charges. In the meantime, the interrogation of the prisoners continued and the German naval officers did not hide their admiration for the exploit of the X6.

From one second to the next, terrible explosions were expected (the crew of the X6 could not help occasionally glancing at their watches). The Germans served the prisoners with hot coffee and spirits and congratulated them. These are the actual words of the official report: " All of them were well treated and given hot coffee and schnapps. Everyone on board the *Tirpitz* expressed great admiration for their bravery."

The British looked at their watches. The charges had been set with an hour's delay. Would the mechanism function? They now thought that they risked being victims of these explosives which they had laid beneath the hull of the *Tirpitz* at the cost of so much difficulty and danger. But mainly they were thinking of the crews of the other midget submarines. What had happened to the X5 and the X7? Had they too been able to deposit their charges and to get away without being spotted? The minutes passed.

For an interminable period, the X7, a steel creature caught in a trap, struggled beneath the hull of the battleship.

07.12—Blew to empty the ballast, and engine full astern.

The X7 freed herself but touched the net and surfaced between two buoys. Dived again immediately. Speed ahead so as not to engage the screw. Caught once more in the net by the bows. After five minutes' manoeuvring, the X7 began to rise. Her compass was faulty and it was impossible to tell their position. She surfaced with engines stopped. " By some extraordinary luck, we must have slipped under the net or through the entrance which had opened for other vessels." Surfaced twenty-five yards from the *Tirpitz* and dived again immediately. The X7 hit the *Tirpitz* at full speed on a level with B gun turret. She glided gently below the hull, released the starboard charge, reversed her engines and released the port charge.

The X7, therefore, had also carried out her mission and the two charges were laid. But the midget had been spotted when she bumped against the hull. The Germans dropped depth charges. Lieutenant Place and his three shipmates heard the explosions, which shook their little vessel. " Dived to five fathoms, changed course and tried to leave. At four fathoms caught again in the net. No compass and practically no air left."

The explosions continued to shake the hull. The men could not help thinking of the other danger which threatened them. The charges she had dropped would explode within the hour and they were still there a few yards away. Not to mention the charges laid by the other X craft which, according to the timetable, should have gone off anywhere after 08.00. The chances of this crew surviving grew more slender but they had not yet lost hope.

" Tried a new technique to try and get out of the net. Engine full speed ahead and then full astern. It was necessary to take advantage of the net's elasticity to get some impetus. We began to see-saw more and more rapidly. For more than half an hour, the X7 was caught in the net, freed and recaught. The compressed air exhausted, the compressor was started."

At 07.40, the X7 freed herself and surfaced between the

buoys. Like the X6 she was too close to the *Tirpitz* for
the guns to be fired but she was raked by machine-guns.
She dived outside the net and settled on the bottom at
twenty fathoms.

(Everything is possible. I suddenly realise that it is possible after all that a description of the struggles of this poor
steel beast caught in a trap might be monotonous to the
reader; that they might hope the description would be
abridged. Personally, I must say that this detailed description arouses my admiration, not only by its object, by its
tragedy, but by its very existence: that during these unbearable and terrifying moments, when the lives of these men
were weighed in the balance, one of them could note down
minute by minute the action of the tragedy. It gives great
food for thought. The original log was lost with the submarine but the Captain, with the help of a survivor,
reconstructed it as soon as he could while the details were
still fresh in his memory. We can consult our history books
in search of similar tragedies. How many shall we find
whose actors retain sufficient self-control to be at the same
time accurate historians?)

"Compressor restarted. Tried to surface to periscope
depth to find our position and move away from the site
of the impending explosions. Caught in the net once more
at four fathoms."

This time it seemed to be the end. In their narrow metal
prison beneath the harsh light of electric lamps, which the
depth charges caused to oscillate, the four men in the X7
looked at each other for a moment in silence. The charges
would explode at any moment. It is inconceivable that
the first explosion would not instantly have destroyed the
X7. Nothing remained but to be resigned and to wait.
But the energy of these men seems to have been inexhaustible. "Full speed ahead," ordered the Captain.

08.12. A terrific explosion. The X7 shot out of net,
surfaced, bobbing about like a cork. And what do we read

at this moment in the reconstructed log book? "The *Tirpitz* was still afloat." The first care of the Captain of the X7 was to look at his target. "The *Tirpitz* was still afloat" (she would soon begin to list and to lose her oil). Once more the X7 dived to the bottom.

"Remained on the bottom to examine our damage." It is incredible. What could Lieutenant Place have hoped for? Fantastic though it may appear, he still hoped to complete his mission—in other words to save his ship and escape from the enemy in order to render his report. Or, if he really no longer entertained this hope, he still wanted to see for himself that it was impossible.

Examination showed that the compass and the depth indicator were definitely out of action. Other vital parts must have been gravely damaged, for the X7 could not now be controlled. Several times she surfaced, dived and re-emerged, each time to be raked by the machine-guns of the *Tirpitz*. Her hull was damaged. Lieutenant Place then decided to abandon ship.

He gave his orders. The Germans continued to drop charges around him and there was no chance of using the individual escape apparatus. The man surfacing would be killed at once. The next time she surfaced, the Captain would open the hatch and they would all leave.

The X7 surfaced quite near a target (a large floating panel used for firing practice). Place leaped out of the tower to let the others pass. Space was so restricted aboard the X ship that he was above the men and it was impossible for him to do anything else. But hardly had he left them than the X7 dived and sank with the rest of the crew. Lieutenant Place took refuge on the target and a launch from the *Tirpitz* came and picked him up. He was taken aboard the battleship and treated like the other prisoners.

At 11.15, another member of the X7's crew, the torpedo-man Aitken, managed to leave the vessel with the help of his life-saving gear. He was picked up. The two other sailors, alas, remained on the bottom.

As for the X5 (commander, Lieutenant H. Henty-Creer), spotted by the German look-outs on entering the fjord at 500 yards from the nets, she was shelled by the *Tirpitz* and subjected to a depth charge attack. She disappeared with her crew.

Thus the main damage inflicted on the *Tirpitz* in the attack by the midget submarines X6 and X7 was as follows: port engine out of action; electric installations out of action; gun turrets A and C shattered by the explosion and completely out of action; all the apparatus for flak fire control put out of gear; numerous water pipes temporarily flooded the electric generator compartment; breaks in the fuel oil pipes, resulting in serious leaks; sundry damage to telemeters, transmission circuits and radar apparatus. The explosions killed one and wounded forty of the battleship's crew.

The first repairs were carried out on the spot. Several depot ships with teams of workmen and material arrived at Alten Fjord. The engineers asked for a 100-ton crane to be sent from Germany. It failed to arrive because of the bad weather.

On the 22nd November, 1943, two months after the attack, the Marinegruppenkommando Nord sent a detailed report to the German High Command, which concluded: "As a result of the successful attack by British midget submarines the *Tirpitz* is out of action for several months."

By the time the repairs were completed, in April, 1944, the Allied air forces had become powerful enough to attack the German battleship at anchor in force.

Badly damaged on several occasions, she sank in Tromsö Fjord on the 12th November, 1944.

The attack by these small submarines had put her out of action for as long as was necessary.

CHAPTER ELEVEN

The Last Raider

THE RUSSIAN CONVOYS, INTERRUPTED
during the summer of 1943 by the length of daylight, which
would have favoured enemy attacks, continued their runs
in the autumn.

The escorts were considerable. They sometimes included
an aircraft carrier, *H.M.S. Fencer* or *Activity*. A supporting force, consisting of cruisers and a covering force including at least a battleship, defended each convoy at a distance.
The best defence of these convoys which sailed after
October, 1943, was the radar which the Allies had perfected.
It now enabled them to detect, even in visibility nil, waves
of enemy aircraft and to despatch the planes of the carrier
to attack them. Very few German machines reached the
convoys and most of them were shot down. Several submarines, also detected by radar, were sunk. This battle of
the Arctic Ocean, which for so long had been an almost
unbearable nightmare for the crews of the merchant ships
and escorts, now became more and more murderous for
the attackers.

On the 26th December, 1943, about 09.30, when convoy
JW 55-B was thirty-five miles S.S.E. of Bear Island sailing
east in a heavy sea and a strong wind, Rear Admiral
Burnett, commanding the supporting cruisers *H.M.S.
Belfast, Norfolk* and *Sheffield,* spotted in the Arctic twilight
far to the south the German battleship *Scharnhorst* sailing
on a northerly course.

Burnett, as we already know, was a man of great decision.

As soon as he had identified the *Scharnhorst* he ordered the convoy to sail north and opened fire with his cruisers. The German battleship replied immediately to the British fire and the battle started.

Until a direct hit has been obtained a naval battle at long distance is not very different from a practice shoot; most of the ship's company have their action stations below decks or in the gun turrets, from which they see nothing of the action. The men on the bridge or at stations where they can see the enemy see nothing but the gun flashes. Their own firing usually prevents them hearing the noise of the enemy's guns or it only reaches their ears like distant thunder. These men see the tall geysers in the water, but an effort of imagination is necessary to establish the relation between the flashes and these spouts, for several seconds separate them, in which there are other flashes and other rocking from the firing of one's own salvoes. However, the bombardment acts on the nerves and the feeling of danger increases.

The engagement between the *Scharnhorst* and the British cruisers had begun at 09.35. The heavy sea made firing inaccurate on both sides. By 10.25, none of the cruisers had been hit. The *Scharnhorst* had probably been hit once. At 10.10 it disappeared in the fog on an easterly course. Admiral Burnett ordered the convoy to continue eastward.

About 12.20 the German battleship reappeared at 12,000 yards, sailing west, *i.e.*, in the direction of the cruisers. She opened fire on them. The three cruisers replied and sailed ahead of her. A shell hit the *Norfolk*, killing and wounding several men. The cruisers continued to sail at full speed for the *Scharnhorst*.

At 12.26 the British officers observing the battleship saw her veer to port. Firing continued on both sides. The British saw the powerful silhouette in profile and then only her stern. She had ceased to take evasive action and was now fleeing at full speed to the east.

The *Scharnhorst* had put to sea on Christmas Day with three destroyers as soon as the convoy had been sighted by the reconnaissance planes from Narvik. Her mission was to intercept and destroy the convoy.

The *Belfast* and the *Sheffield* each had twelve 5·7-inch guns, the *Norfolf* eight 8-inch. The *Scharnhorst* had nine 11-inch and twelve 6-inch. These gun figures are not enough to establish the comparison of the forces. Other elements had to be taken into consideration, some appreciable others not. As a battleship, the *Scharnhorst* was indubitably more powerful and better armoured than Burnett's cruisers. Theoretically the latter could not inflict definite damage in an exchange of gunfire, while it, on the contrary, could destroy them. The *Scharnhorst*, however, broke off the action for the following reason: she did not know exactly what was facing her. She was entitled to fear that the three cruisers she could see were only part of an important naval squadron, including carriers and perhaps battleships. On this principle one might say that any ship that saw an enemy vessel might refuse combat on the pretext that it might be the advanced guard of a large squadron. That is true. The aggressive spirit of the British warship's commanders in the tactical field was far superior to that of their adversaries, and this weighed heavily in the balance. But the feeling of inferiority which made the *Scharnhorst* flee on the 26th December, 1943, partly originated from an empirical truth: the German capital ships in the event of an encounter always risked finding themselves outnumbered. By the end of 1943, a battleship which had no air cover (carriers or shore stations in the proximity) nor a perfected radar, was in fact an archaic and outdated vessel. The only operation it could envisage, without taking enormous risks, was a surprise attack on an inferior adversary, such as the convoy defended by only small escort vessels, to destroy it and flee before the intervention of the supporting and covering forces. Without the full element of surprise the blow would fail.

26th December, 15.00. The battle had been over since 12.35. The *Scharnhorst* was now sailing S.S.E. at her full speed in the heavy sea—twenty-seven knots. The three British cruisers followed her on a parallel course. In spite of their theoretical equal speed (thirty-two knots) they lost distance—the disadvantage of a light as opposed to a heavy vessel when sailing into the sea. The afternoon was drawing to a close and night fell. Captain Hintze, in command of the battleship, and Rear-Admiral Bey, flying his flag aboard, must have thought that although their mission was a failure they could at least bring the *Scharnhorst* back to port. That was something. Coming on top of the im-mobilisation of the *Tirpitz* by the midget submarines, the loss of the *Scharnhorst* would have a catastrophic effect in Germany.

Now had these two German naval officers possessed radar comparable with that of the Allies they would doubtless have carried out quite different tactics. They would not have continued to follow their course towards Alten Fjord on an S.S.E. course for they would have seen on the luminous dial the large unit which was now advancing from the S.S.W. to head them off. This large unit was the battleship *H.M.S. Duke of York*, 35,000 tons with ten 14-inch guns. *H.M.S. Duke of York*, in which Admiral Fraser, successor to Admiral Tovey as C.in-C. Home Fleet, flew his flag, together with the cruiser *H.M.S. Jamaica* and several destroyers consolidated the covering force of convoy JW 55-B. As soon as he had sighted the *Scharnhorst*, Admiral Burnett warned Admiral Fraser by radio and the latter immediately set a course to head off the German battleship. From the start of his chase Burnett had detached four destroyers from the convoy's escort, giving them orders to keep in contact with the *Scharnhorst* at all cost. These destroyers, *H.M.S. Savage, Saumarez, Scorpion* and *Stord*, were new ships which had only been in com-mission a few months. They had reached thirty-six knots on their trials. These greyhounds, moreover, were extremely solid, although their displacement was only 1,600 tons. Their race with the *Scharnhorst* in this heavy sea will always remain a great naval occasion. They kept the battleship in sight while twilight lasted and when night fell followed it on their radar screens. They reported every quarter of an hour to Burnett, who passed the message on to Fraser. The latter at last picked up the *Scharnhorst* in his radar.

The German battleship, unaware of all this, continued to sail S.S.E.

On board the *Duke of York* the central radar reported each minute the distance of the *Scharnhorst* to the bridge. At 16.50, in complete darkness, Fraser fired a salvo of star shells from 11,000 yards at the invisible enemy. It was the marvel of radar precision. The silhouette of the *Scharnhorst* appeared on the sea at exactly the position foreseen.

The German battleship, taken by surprise, veered to port. Fraser set a parallel course and gave orders to open fire. The thunder of her 14-inch guns shook the great vessel, immediately followed by salvoes from the secondary armament, sixteen 5·25-inch guns. The *Jamaica* began to fire with her twelve 6-inch guns.

In a note dated 3rd September, 1939, Admiral Raeder made the following observations: " It is obvious that the German Navy is by no means ready to make war against Great Britain. Our surface forces are so inferior in number and power to those of the British Fleet that all they can do is to show how to die bravely and thus lay the foundations for a future reconstruction." The inequality between the surface squadrons had increased. The ship's company of the *Scharnhorst* had nothing left except to show that they could die bravely.

She replied to the enemy's fire and defended herself well, not only in her firing but in her manoeuvring. After each salvo of her nine 11-inch guns she put her helm hard over to port to present the narrow target of her stern to the enemy, then came back on the starboard tack, fired another broadside and repeated the manoeuvre. The *Duke of York* and the *Jamaica* fired by radar. In a calm sea this firing would have been impressive, but in the swell which was still violent the battle was prolonged. Fires were now visible aboard the German battleship, which continued to fire. Her shells passed over the *Duke of York*.

At 18.06 a direct hit damaged the *Scharnhorst's* engines. Her speed fell to twenty knots and she ceased firing. Fraser broke off his fire and moved in closer.

At 18.30 the crew of the *Duke of York* and the *Jamaica* saw the *Scharnhorst* reopen fire at a nearby target. By the light of their star shells they could see the oulines of several destroyers pressing home their attack on the battleship. They were the *Savage*, the *Saumarez*, the *Scorpion* and the *Stord*. As soon as they had seen the *Scharnhorst* reduce speed they manoeuvred to come in from ahead and carry out a torpedo attack from 1,000 yards. The *Stord*, flying the Norwegian flag, streaked in so boldly that the spectators thought she would ram the battleship. Their torpedoes launched, they made a classic withdrawal behind a smoke screen. One of them, the *Saumarez*, received a direct hit, killing and wounding several of the crew.

But the *Scharnhorst* had received three torpedoes. Continuing to fire at the *Duke of York*, she sailed east more and more slowly. At 19.00 Fraser opened fire again. It was the *coup-de-grâce*. Fires raged on the battleship, the magazines blew up and a monstrous firework display lit up the night. Then the floating brazier went round in circles like a blind man : her rudder was blocked.

The Allied vessels drew in and surrounded her with their guns. They switched on their searchlights. The dying ship continued to fire an occasional shot to show that she would not surrender.

19.35. Admiral Fraser gave orders to the *Belfast* and the *Jamaica* to sink her with torpedoes. Several dull explosions and the burning *Scharnhorst* sank under the light of the searchlights.

197

Of her complement of 1,900 men, thirty-six escaped.

The story of the Russian convoys draws to a close.

Not that the traffic ceased on the Arctic Ocean. It continued, but in conditions which belong in the realms of statistics rather than in literature. From the beginning of 1944, the Admiralty used both sea routes to Russia, the Arctic Ocean and the Persian Gulf, merely taking into account the unloading capacity of the ports. The destruction of the *Scharnhorst* had virtually put an end to the martyrdom of the convoys and their escorts. The runs were still unpleasant on account of the cold and the bad weather, but air and U-boat attacks grew rarer and utterly incapable of stopping them. The Allies had now gone over to the offensive. The surface raiders no longer left port, and the most formidable of them was soon to be sunk skulking in its haven.

At the end of March, 1944, as soon as the Allies learned that the *Tirpitz* had been repaired, a naval force was sent to Norway consisting of the heavy carriers *H.M.S. Victorious* and *Furious,* the light carriers *H.M.S. Searcher, Pursuer, Fencer* and *Emperor,* protected by units of the Home Fleet. On 3rd April sixty aircraft from these carriers dropped a hundred bombs on Alten Fjord. On fire and damaged, the *Tirpitz* still did not sink, in August four new bombing attacked destroyed Alten Fjord and several other German bases in Norway ; but the *Tirpitz* was still afloat. At the beginning of September, a formation of heavy Lancaster bombers flying from Great Britain, taking on ammunition in Russia, dropped 6,000 tons of bombs on Alten Fjord on the 13th. The *Tirpitz* which had had time to put out a dense cloud of smoke once more survived this murderous attack. On 25th October, the Russians having captured Kirkenes, the Germans decided to tow their battleship to Tromsö. This is where the *coup de grâce* was dealt, on 12th November, 1944. Hit by two six-ton bombs which pierced her armour plating before exploding, ripping her open to a length of thirty yards, she capsized and sank within three minutes.

The Norwegian bases from which the Luftwaffe took off, those from which the U-boats and surface craft sailed were blitzed, destroyed and evacuated. Thus ended the long air-sea battle of the Arctic for the convoys to get through.

In every war one hears mention of places situated in regions of the globe where nothing happens in peacetime. Today, as in 1939, the Arctic Ocean route is deserted. The icebergs collide in the solitude of the polar night, but the endless-day lights up an expanse where no ship sails and the sky is empty of aircraft. Let us hope that for long these desolate waters will remain at peace. For it suffices to look at them on the map—not the maps we usually consult but on a globe—to see what the re-opening of the Arctic theatre of war signifies in our era of planetary strategy.

THE END.